Content

Pfeil Magazine 17 – High

1	10 Years Clean	Katie Della-Valle
2	Editorial	Anja Dietmann
4	We Made It	Lila de Magalhaes, Michael Kent
5	LECTURE THREE The Body in Today's Reproductive Crisis	Silvia Federici
7	27.11.2022, 15.03.2023, 08.08.2020	Masha Silchenko
10	I Grew Out of That Place	Cecilia Gentili, Michelle Esther O'Brien
17	High Art	Sands Murray-Wassink
18	Fear	Penny Goring
19	Marie's Story	Claire DeVoogd
20	Traffic Lights at Eye Level	Paul Niedermayer
23	Up There and Down There: On the Low and High Levels of Drugs	Jakob Tanner
27	Palast der Republik–Burj Khalifa	Jasmin Werner
30	The View	Jane Joritz-Nakagawa
31	Toad Retreat	Gerrit Frohne-Brinkmann
35	Radiation With Benefits	Lucy Beech, Riar Rizaldi
39	ESPD55	Marina Pinsky
43	Where the Waves Rise Higher	Tina Kämpe
44	Nanjing Lukou International Airport	Tang Han
45	Towers of Hope	Christiane Blattmann
51	Backstage Boo 1, 2, 3	Bod Mellor
54	Müde	Moesari
55	The Weak Lips of a Woman	Cordula Ditz
57	Thighs	Jan Matthé
58	About Turn, Resounds, Decays	Katy Lewis Hood, Leah Jun Oh, Jac Common
60	Botanomancy	Paige Emery
61	Recent Dreams	Alejandra López
65	Unruly Women on Planes, Nameplates, and Goats	Nina Kuttler

Editor: Anja Dietmann
Copy Editor: Stacy Skolnik
Layout: JMMP – Julian Mader, Max Prediger
Print: Pöge Druck, Leipzig

Publisher: Montez Press
Unit 29, Penarth Centre
Penarth Street
SE15 1TR London
United Kingdom

ISBN: 978-3-945247-27-3

© Copyright 2023 Montez Press and the authors. All rights reserved.
No part of this publication may be reproduced without permission in writing by the authors and the publisher.
p. 18, "Fear" as part of Penny Goring's poem collection *Fail Like Fire*, Arcadia Missa Edition 2022;
p. 48, picture of Robert Walser in courtesy of KEYSTONE / ROBERT WALSER FOUNDATION BERN.

Lila de Magalhaes, Michael Kent

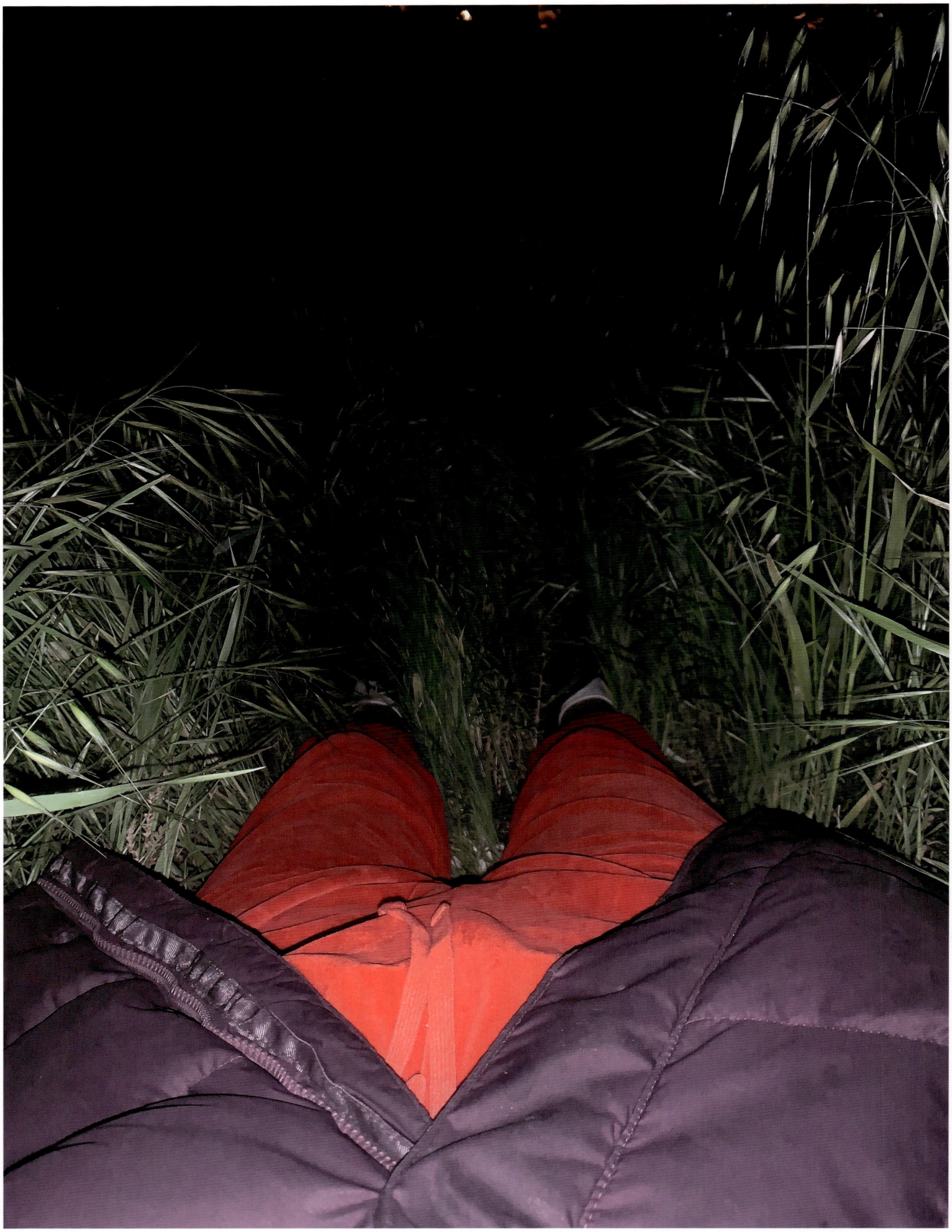

LECTURE THREE The Body in Today's Reproductive Crisis

Silvia Federici

"LECTURE THREE The Body in Today's Reproductive Crisis" is part of *Beyond the Periphery of the Skin: Rethinking, Remaking, and Reclaiming the Body in Contemporary Capitalism*, published by PM Press, www.pmpress.org, Oakland 2020.

Changing our body, regaining control over our sexuality and reproductive capacity, is to change the material conditions of our lives. To what extent this principle must guide our individual and collective activities is shown by the crisis that we are currently experiencing in the US despite the intense feminist activism of the last half of the century. It is a crisis that has many dimensions: sexual, procreative, ecological, medical, cognitive, all rooted however in economic and social developments that have drastically reduced the time and resources at our disposal and increased our anxiety about the future and the violence to which we are exposed. Capitalism's old dream to lengthen the workday, reduce wages, and maximize the unpaid labor accumulated is fully realized today in the United States. Indeed, what Marx described as the "general law of capital accumulation"[1]—the relative impoverishment of workers, the constant creation of surplus/disposable populations, the deskilling of most available jobs, overwork in the presence of a massive number of unemployed "compe[lling] those who are employed to furnish more labor" (Marx 1990, 793)—is the tendency governing economic and social life, and so are the attendant problems of mass indigence, homelessness, and the deepening of inequalities and institutional violence.

Life, indeed, for the majority of people, and women above all, approximates today the Hobbesian description of the state of nature: it is nasty, brutish, and short. Well-to-do Americans may now live into their nineties, but for the rest of us life expectancy is declining, with suicides and deaths from drug overdose also at a record high.[2] Suicides are growing among all sectors of the population, women included. There were over forty-seven thousand recorded suicides in 2017 in the United States, and we will never know how many—among older people—have let themselves die, unrecorded, because a life spent battling with poverty and isolation had no meaning for them. Added to the thousands of deaths from drug overdose, gun violence, police killing, and untreated diseases, they form a worrisome landscape that we cannot ignore in our political work.

In this context, I want to highlight those aspects of this crisis that are particularly relevant for rethinking a feminist agenda. The first are overwork, debt, lack of security, life as constant tension and exhaustion, always thinking of the next task, resulting in health problems, depression, and, as we have seen, an increase in the number of suicides.

Contrasting with the congratulatory, celebratory appraisals, by the United Nations and liberal feminist organizations, of the great steps toward emancipation women have presumably made, the situation today of the majority of the female population could not be bleaker. Undoubtedly, today we are much less tied to the family and to men than in the past. The traditional family is no longer the norm: marriage is at a record low, and most women today have a waged job or even two, even when they have young children. But we are paying a high price for the relative autonomy we have gained. Nothing has changed in the workplace. As we know, most jobs assume that workers are free from family commitments or have someone at home taking care of housework. But as 40 percent of women are the sole providers for their families and the rest have partners who are also employed, domestic work does not disappear when we work outside the home. It is done at night, on weekends, at times that should be devoted to resting and other activities. This means that for many women the workweek averages from sixty to ninety hours, like at the peak of the Industrial Revolution, starting at six in the morning and ending at nine in the evening. Reports abound of women saying that they have hardly any time for themselves and live on the verge of a nervous breakdown, constantly worrying, constantly feeling rushed, anxious, or guilty, especially for not having enough time with the children, or having stress-related health problems starting with depression. Even so, most women have had to reduce the amount of housework they do, which means that essential tasks go unattended, as no services have replaced the work once done by them. Meanwhile programs that could address these problems are being cut.

One would hope that the crisis on the domestic front may be compensated by the satisfactions women may gain from employment. But for most women, working outside the home means to be imprisoned in jobs that destroy their bodies and minds—jobs where you stand up, all day, in shops, airports, and supermarkets, often alone waiting for clients, selling goods that salaries cannot buy, or being chained to a computer screen in box-like, windowless offices. It means paying for daycare and transport and having to depend on fast food at a time when we should be vigilant, given the spread of pesticides and transgenic products and the growth of obesity all around us, including among children. Add that many jobs do not provide paid sick leave or paid maternity leave and that the cost of daycare averages $10,000 a year.

This is not to say that we should not take jobs outside the home. But it is to recognize that "choice" and control over our bodies cannot be achieved only by reducing the number of the children we have or gaining the right not to have children and working for a wage. It is building the power to force the state to relinquish the resources that we need for our families and communities, so that we do not have to take two jobs, spend all our time worrying about money, or give up our children in surrogacy or adoption because we cannot support them. "Going out of the home" and "fighting for equality" is not enough. We must reappropriate resources, work less, regain control of our lives, and take responsibility for the well-being of a broader world than that of our families.

Adding to economic poverty is the poverty of living in a world in which, wherever we turn, we see signs of death. The birds are leaving our skies, rivers are turning into chemical dumps, we have no time for love, friendship, and learning. Capitalism has made us lose sight of the magic of life. In a meeting I met a woman who works as a doula.[3] This is a practice that comes from the reproductive justice movement. It is the idea that women who have a history of mistreatment by the medical profession should not to go the hospital to give birth alone but should go with an advocate. It is a step toward reconstituting the community of women that was once present at the time of birth. This woman was asked, "What is magic?" And her answer was: "Go see a woman giving birth. There's nothing more magical: the way the rhythms of the mother coordinate with the rhythms of the child is simply magical." But today we give birth on an assembly line. As Meg Fox (1989, 125–29) described it in her article on subjective and objective time in childbirth, today "the time of labor is counted." Labor has become "mere production." The emphasis is on efficiency, as in a time-motion study. Births are not felt. Children are pulled out of sensationless bodies. Giving birth is reduced to a mechanical process.

Nature too is magical. One day the soil is brown and next flowers are generated from it of all colors. How these colors or the forms of the flowers were produced by this same soil no science has yet explained. Magic is the world seen in all its creativity and self-movement. It is around us, but we do not recognize it. We have lost the capacity to relate to it. Attraction among people is also magical. Renaissance scholars spoke of the "harmony of the spheres." They believed that the universe was kept together by an amorous force—similar in its effects to the force of gravity. They believed that the power of "attraction" kept everything in its place and this was as present among humans as it was among the stars. This view of the universe as something living, where everything is interconnected gives power to our struggle. It is an antidote against the cynical view that it is worthless to strive to change the world because "it is too late," "things are too far gone," and we should not get too close to others because we cannot trust them and should think of ourselves first.

Efforts to recuperate our relation with others and with nature are not missing. Women, especially those from indigenous communities, are forming urban gardens, seed banks, they bury their placentas in the earth to remind their children of their ties with the soil. In the US as well, in urban settings, gardens as well as time banks are spreading and other forms of "commoning" once limited to radical groups. We are becoming aware that when we lose our relation to the land we lose much more than an economic resource. As Native Americans have always known, in losing the land we lose our knowledge, our history, our culture. As Marx (1988, 75–76) recognized, nature is our inorganic body, an extension of ourselves. Thus, the death of the earth is our death. When a forest is cut, when the seas are polluted and thousands of whales come to the shore, we too die. Thus, there are now many women's organizations that are working to recuperate older forms of knowledge about herbs and plants.

There is also a growing awareness of the barbaric suffering that is inflicted on animals in almost every branch of industry. Animals too are being turned into machines. In barns across the country that now resemble industrial plants or, more appropriately, animal concentration camps, the lights are kept on day and night so that chickens will produce greater volumes of eggs. It is the same with female pigs. Millions of animals are raised solely to be eaten. They are not seen as living beings but meat producing machines, engineered in such a way that some will never get up on their feet before being driven to a slaughterhouse because the flesh in their bodies is heavier than their legs can support.[4] No wonder we have so many cancers. We live in a poisoned earth and feed on animals that since their birth have been horribly tortured—taking into our own bodies all the poison that their agony has produced.

As I said, we are beginning to develop a revulsion against the Nazi-like cruelty that is inflicted on millions of living beings in the name of satisfying our desires. The rise of Animal Liberation has been an important contribution to revolutionary politics, and so is the silent revolution taking place among many young people across the world who are turning vegetarian or vegan, some perhaps out of concern for their well-being but many out of revulsion against the suffering that the satisfaction of our desire for meat requires.

Yet much remains to be done. Despite so many social movements, social struggles, and so much celebration of human rights, we have not been able to address the main crisis on which American society has been built—the consequences of centuries of slavery and genocide, which like an ocean of blood affects and distorts everything that is done on this continent. What would a feminist movement be like that placed not just the struggle against racism, but also against the institutions that generate it, at the top of its agenda as an intolerable social crime?

Racism in all its forms is so deeply ingrained in white American and European society that extirpating it will require a long revolutionary process. But a feminist movement can mobilize against the policies and institutions that support racial discrimination and the new forms of enslavement to which not only black people but also Latino and immigrant communities are subjected. We also need a movement fighting for the abolition of the death penalty as well as the carceral system and the militarism permeating every aspect of our lives. A feminist objective must be also the liberation of the thousands of women incarcerated in the US—the largest percentage of female prisoners in any country, who are imprisoned mostly for "survival crimes," such as selling sex or forging checks, and because pregnancy, in the case of low-income women and black women, has been increasingly criminalized.

We need a feminist movement that mobilizes in solidarity with our children, whose lives are also daily threatened. There is now some concern for the senseless shootings of kids of all ages in schools and kindergartens, though not enough clearly to change policies relating to gun control. Also, the abuses perpetrated for decades by priests in churches and sacristies are receiving some attention. But feminists have yet to mobilize against the violence to which children are routinely subjected by state institutions, often under the guise of protecting children from their parents, and in the home.

If we refuse the violence done to us, with more reasons we must refuse the violence done to our children. We need to valorize our children, looking at them as companions rather than inferior beings. Children have not yet interiorized the defeats and conventions that shape our relations with others as we become adults and can spot immediately what is false, artificial. Only through years of conditioning do we learn to hide and simulate. Thus, there is much we can learn from them.

Putting an end to all forms of violence done to children is an urgent matter, as childhood is in a state of emergency in the US schools are becoming prisons, with metal detectors and guards at the door. Creative programs are eliminated from their curricula, at least in the public schools. And at home there is less and less time for children. We should not be surprised, then, if they are unhappy and rebel. Instead this rebellion is described as mental illness and medicalized. This is easier and more profitable than recognizing the reasons for children's discontent. It would be a revolution indeed if, instead of spending a trillion dollars to refurbish the nuclear system, the US government spent a trillion dollars to make sure that our schools stimulate the creativity of our children. This is a good feminist project and a good feminist demand!

Notes:
1) Marx, *Capital*, vol. 1, pt. 7, chap. 25.
2) As reported by Shehab Khan, in the *Independent* (November 29, 2018) "Suicides in the US hit a record level in years, prompting a decline in life expectancy." Deaths due to overdose also climbed, surpassing seventy thousand in 2017. According to the Center for Disease Control and Prevention, up to seven hundred thousand people in the United States died from a drug overdose between 1999 and 2017, involving opioids. Every day an average of 130 people die of overdose.
3) On the significance of the role of doulas as advocated for women giving birth, see Alana Apfel, *Birth Work as Care Work* (2016).
4) A powerful, poignant denunciation of the cruelties inflicted on animals in the industrial farms where they are raised by the thou- sands before being brought to the slaughterhouse is in Sunaura Taylor's *Beasts of Burden* (2017), which, while exposing the living hell on which the food industry is built, shows that the degradation of animals "has contributed to unspeakable violence against humans" (107).

Masha Silchenko

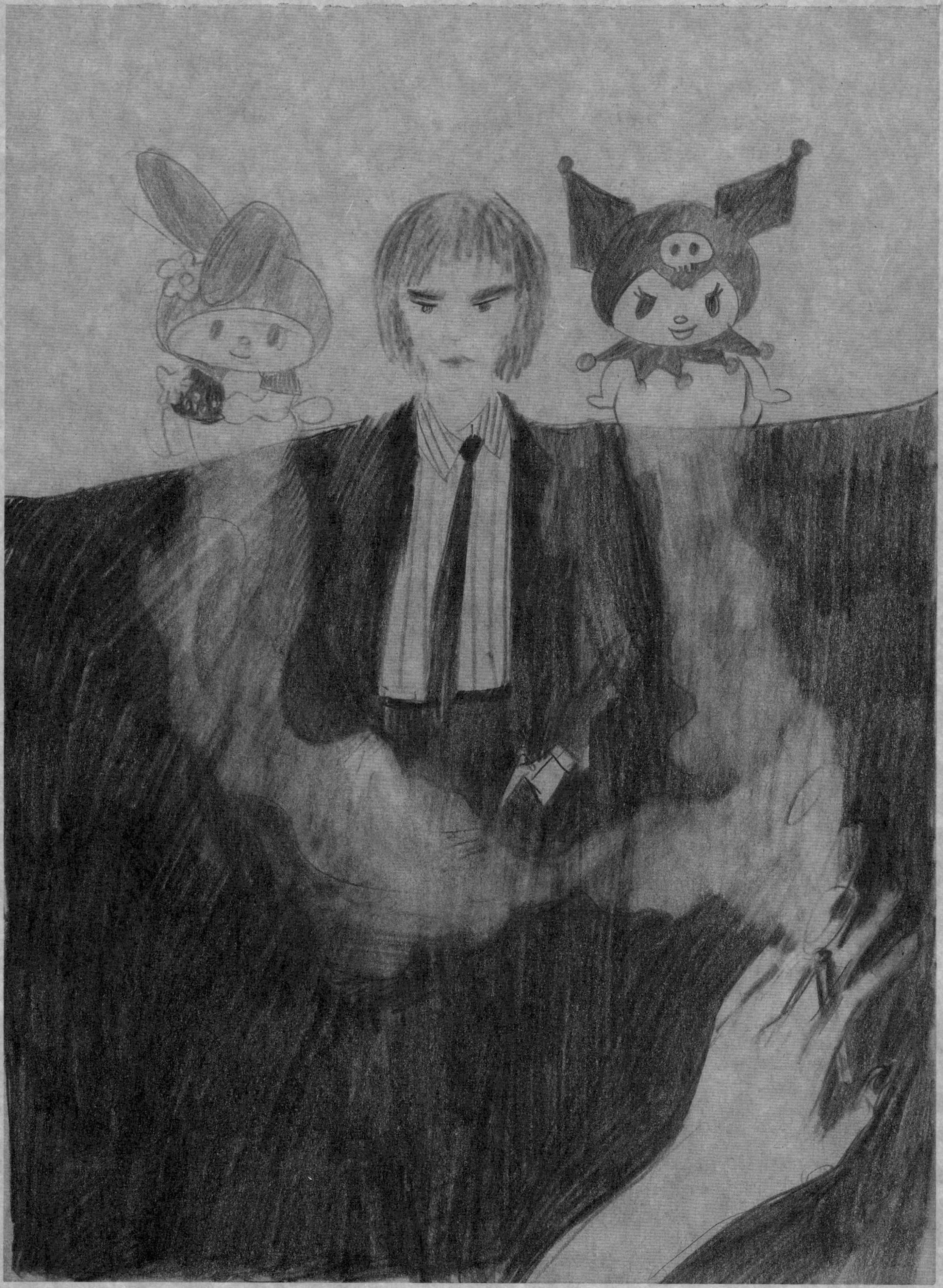

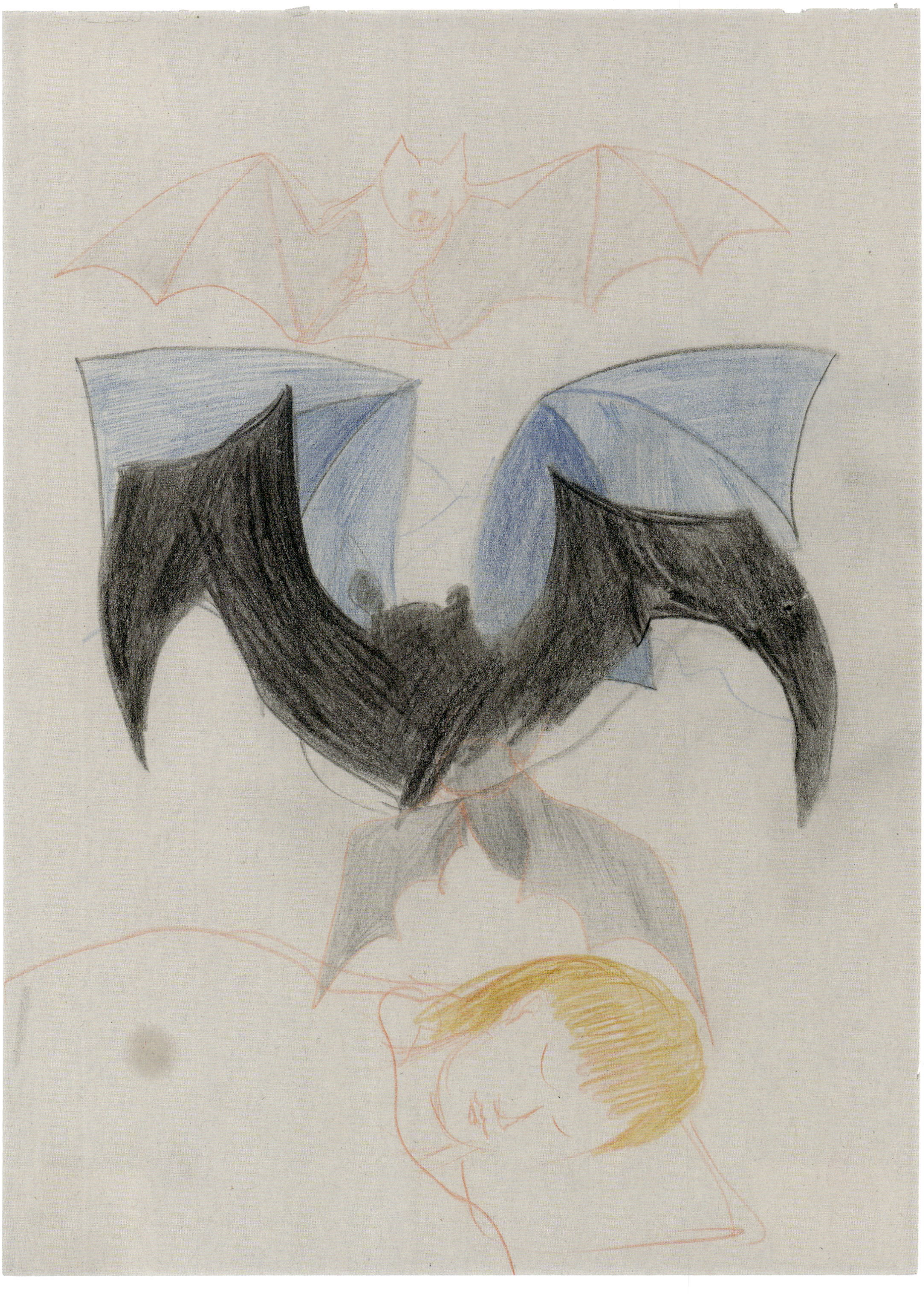

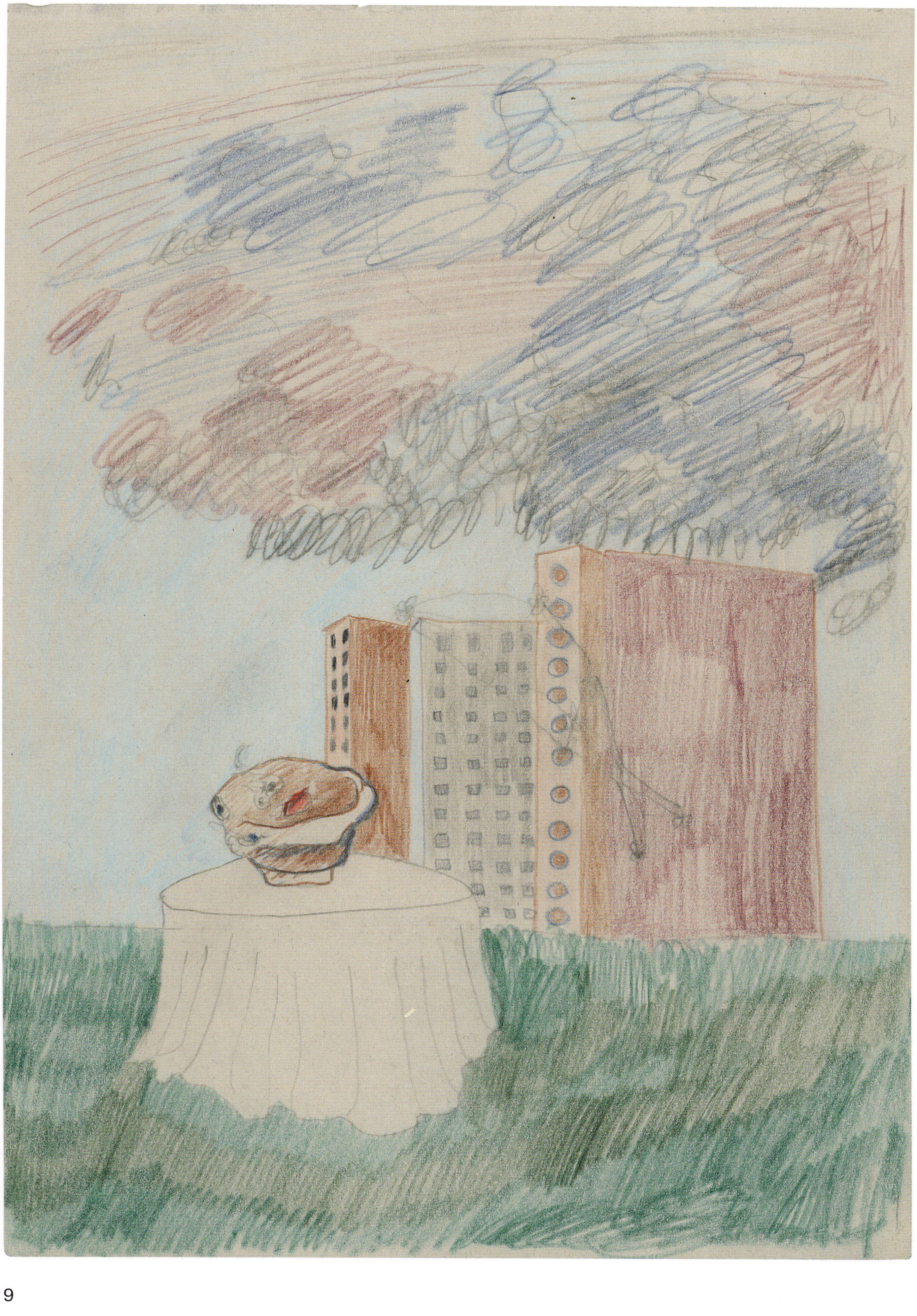

9

I Grew Out of That Place

Michelle Esther O'Brien (MB), Cecilia Gentili (CG)

In this wide-ranging interview, Cecilia Gentili reflects on the relationships and experiences that inform her story of struggle, resilience, and joy. Cecilia recounts her childhood and adolescence in Gálvez, Argentina, describing complex family dynamics and early experiences with gender nonconformity and transphobia. Cecilia's journey also includes years in Miami and New York City facing addiction, homelessness, incarceration, and life under threat of deportation as an undocumented immigrant. Finally, she considers her professional success as an organizer and advocate for the trans community and beyond.

MB   Hello, my name is Michelle O'Brien and I will be having a conversation with Cecilia Gentili for the New York City Trans Oral History Project in collaboration with the New York Public Library's Community Oral History Project. This is an oral history project centered on the experiences of trans identifying people. It is June 9, 2017, and this is being recorded in the offices of Gay Men's Health Crisis. Hello.

CG   Hi, how are you?

MB   I'm doing very well. How are you feeling today?

CG   A little tired, but good. I'm excited about doing this, and I think it's a great project.

MB   Tell me about your job here.

CG   Well, I'm the Director of Policy here at GMHC. I do everything that has to do with making sure that changes in policy or implementation of policies in a city level or in a state level, and at a national level, are the best policies for what we believe is the right of different communities like the HIV community, women, immigrants, trans people, people that use drugs, sex workers—those are all the good things we believe in, we just make sure that everything that has to do with policy is relevant to what we believe is right. So, that's kind of what I do.

MB   I'm going to ask you some questions about your life up to this point, and if we can get to it, I'd love to hear a lot more about your job. So, where did you grow up?

CG   I grew up in the city of Gálvez, in the state of Santa Fe in the nation of Argentina. The Republic of Argentina.

MB   And when were you born?

CG   I was born on January 31, of 1972, which was a very hot summer, sweaty day. And I celebrate it now here usually with snow to my knees, which doesn't make sense to me yet. After so many years living here, I still can't put my birthday with the cold.

MB   What was your family like? What kind of work did they do?

CG   My family, I had a father that was a butcher—

MB   Did he own a shop or was he an employee?

CG   He owned a shop, and he also had a small farm, and in that farm, he would have cows that he would then send to be slaughtered, and sold the meat. My mother, until I was about seven years old, was a cook in a men's school. And then she was a cleaning lady in a music school. She seems to excel at ironing, so she would iron for some rich folks that needed somebody to iron clothes.

MB   What was your first memory?

CG   I'm forgetting my brother. I have a brother who is seven years older than me, and he still lives in Argentina. My first memory was at my grandmother's house, where I would spend weekends and holidays, and my first memory is a tangerine tree. It's me playing under a tangerine tree and going up the tangerine tree and eating tangerines and everything that was around that tangerine tree.

MB   Did it smell?

CG   Like nothing else in the world. It is my favorite smell. Tangerines and orange, also. Kind of like, citrus is my favorite smell. It may have something to do with that. The tangerine tree was an amazing place to play and have fun as a child.

MB   What were you like as a child?

CG   I was terrible, and I was lonely. I was a child that really enjoyed playing by herself, and I think it had to do with the fact that I kind of realized at a very early age that other children didn't want to play with me because my gender issues, I guess? So, I made a clear decision that I would play by myself. Kind of picturing a child playing by themselves may sound kind of sad, but I was a very happy child all the time. I don't know if many children do this, but I was known for eating dirt. And that wasn't a good thing for my mom and my grandmother. Everybody kind of freaked out because I would be eating dirt.

MB   They got mad at you?

CG   They would get really mad at me, and at the time it was the '70s. There wasn't so many directions about what was okay to do. So, I would get spanked a lot for eating dirt, and other things.

MB   You mentioned that other children didn't like you because of your gender.

CG   Yes.

MB   What was your gender like at that time? How did it come out?

CG   Well, another part of my first memory is that when I was talking about my grandma's house and the tangerine tree, I think I was around four years old, I was being kicked out of the girl's bathroom. One day I went to school and then they told me, "don't come to class. You have to go to the principal's office." And even if you're five, you know that the principal's office is some shit that's going down, and that you did something wrong. I was very scared, and I have a clear memory of walking there thinking, "What happened, why am I going to the principal's office?" And I remember being little and reaching for the doorknob, and having to make an effort, to just push and open it. I saw the principal, my teacher, my mother, and these two women on each side that after the fact I learned were a psychologist and a psychiatrist. We had a meeting where they showed me pictures of what I know now was female and male genitalia, and they asked me which one was mine. I kind of chose the one that was a penis, because that was the one that looked like mine. They explained to me that penises were what boys have, and that's why it was a boy's bathroom to go to, and that I shouldn't go to the girl's bathroom anymore. I thought they were absolutely crazy. There's also other parts of this story. The area that I lived as a child in Argentina was known as an area where there was UFO activities, with those marks in the corn fields. I remember jumping on my bike and trying to find if there were any UFO activities. One time, driving to my grandmother's house with my brother on a very dark night, we went through a railroad, and my brother told me, "I have something to tell you, but you have to promise me that you're not going to tell mom or dad about this." And I said, "What happened?" He said, "Did you see that railroad that we just passed? That's where we found you five years ago. You were a baby." And I'd say, "Was I in a basket?" And he said "No, no basket." I said, "Was I wrapped in a blanket?" And he said "No, you were there naked." And I started crying. He said, "Don't cry, I just want you to know that you're not our family, that you were found." During the rest of the trip to my grandma's house, I put two and two together and I thought, this is an area with a lot of UFO activities. I am a girl with a fucking dick. And I was found there? I know what happened here, I was left by mistake by a UFO, and I thought that somewhere there would be a planet where all girls could have penises like me. I told that to my grandmother, who totally entertained the idea, and we waited for a couple of nights to see if any UFO would come back to get me. She was ready to let me go back there, and she waited with me until late at night, helped me prepare a little backpack in case they would come to rescue me. It was so cool that she did that.

MB What was the political context in Argentina like at the time?

CG It was one of the worst dictatorships. Parts of my family were more involved in politics. Because of that, that was a conversation that was always on the table. But most of the people didn't really know what was happening, didn't really know that people were being kidnapped and killed and that pregnant people were being kidnapped and their children were stolen from them and then they were killed, and those children were sold, and everything that was not totally in line with the dictatorship that was going on, was simply eliminated. You were against the dictatorship, you were going to disappear and be killed. Most people didn't even know or didn't want to know, which I'm not saying this in any kind of judgmental way—many people don't want to know, or they don't want to talk about these kind of things, because it's a way to deal with the problem. My family did talk about it because many members of my family were very political.

MB Were they on the left or connected to the government?

CG Most of my family members were on the right, but also at the same time it was this confrontation in-between parties. My mom's family, who were the poor ones—I don't know why they were conservatives. My dad's family who wasn't rich, but had more resources, they were liberals. So, it was an issue between families. And in my mom's family, my aunt was married to a person that was very politically involved, and they were always hiding. There were periods of time that we didn't see them, and we didn't know if they were alive or not because they had to hide. Very, very traumatic times, and it took me a long time to understand that a lot of my family members, they weren't just against my persona, they were just very scared of what could happen and what happened to people like me that didn't conform to gender or sexuality or had a big mouth, like I was known for having. It was very problematic—a very horrible time. People are still being found nowadays. Last year one of these children that were conceived under the dictatorship, which the mother is still missing and most likely is to be dead because she was killed, and this child was sold or given to a family, to a movement that is called Madres de Plaza de Mayo, they're still looking for their grandchildren. Last year they found one, and it was a big event in Argentina. The political climate in the country was very conflicting until 1984, which I was 12 years old when we found a way to go back to democracy. The fact that Argentina found democracy in 1984 didn't really affect me much in a way that people kind of perceive it. I think that democracy was just a name that was dropped into a nation that was mentally living in a dictatorship. It's not that democracy comes, and everybody changes their ways, way of thinking, and understand what democracy is. Since 1984 I live in a democracy around people with dictatorship mentality. That is as bad as living in a dictatorship. It was hard. I was 12, I was a very queer person, we found this idea of democracy and I learned what gay people were, because people started talking about it. But the ideas were incomprehensible, and very, very oppressive.

MB Did you encounter any trans people or gender non-conforming people when you were growing up?

CG No. I had no idea what it was. And I always thought like I was crazy. So, I try not to think about that, because I thought that was some kind of mental illness and every time I tried to talk about that, that was how it was addressed. As, no, you are crazy. That's what it is. But I always knew that I was a girl. I just felt I shouldn't talk about that. At age 12, I was attracted to boys at the time. And so, around age 10, 12, I came across the idea of being gay. I felt, this is closer. If they say that I'm not a girl, maybe I am a boy, and there's some boys that like boys. And I was sexually active with boys and everything, but at age 12 I came out to my mom and said I was a gay boy. She had a hard time with it, which doesn't make sense. You had a meeting when your child was five because your child was going to the girl's bathroom. Is it surprising that at age 12 that child comes out as something? For example, this is one of my mother's phrases that I cannot get out of my head. She would say, "We're going to your aunt today. Please don't ask for anything to eat. Unless you are extremely thirsty, don't ask for anything to drink. Unless you really, really need to use the bathroom, don't ask to go to the bathroom. Please, please, when you talk, hold your hands together." And I said "Why?" And she said, "Because when you talk, you move them too much, like in a very flamboyant, feminine way, and I hate it." So, with all these signs, I don't know why she had a hard time when I came out as gay. Again, I came to understand now that the people really didn't have an issue with me, my sexuality or coming out as gay… They were scared because gay people were just killed. There were no rights or anything. I think it wasn't just that they were against me, they were just very scared about it. I came out as gay at age 12. And then when I moved to a big city called Rosario at age 17, I met the first trans person there, and it was this realization of somebody else is like me in the world.

MB What were they like?

CG Gorgeous. She was gorgeous, and she's still gorgeous. Although my ideas of beauty have changed dramatically through the years, at the time I thought she was the most beautiful woman ever.

MB Where did you meet her?

CG I met her in a bar. She had long, blond hair, big breasts, big hips and ass, and a small nose. Very kind of Barbie-like kind of beauty, which now I kind of like, ugh, but at the time she was everything that I thought was beautiful. I told her that I wanted to be like her. And she looked at me and she said, "Okay. But you know how this life is?" And I said, "No." She said, "Well, if you want to be like me, you need to know that you're going to be a whore, you're going to get high, and you're going to die young." And I said, "Where do I sign? This is what I want." At the same time, I met with this older person who was so advanced into gender because she would live as a very feminine man—I guess. It was some transness, but it wasn't totally focused on the feminine spectrum. It was what you would call somebody, gender bender, or genderfluid person, and she helped me in ways that not many people have helped me in my life. She also had me in her house and taught me a lot. She showed compassion and became what was my first family of choice.

MB How did she help you?

CG Well, we would do shows in bars. I wasn't really gifted with being talented at dancing or lip synching or singing. I was kind of funny. And for some reason, people liked me. I'm not going to say that I was pretty—but I was very well put-together. So, we started making a lot of money working in clubs and in bars. Not only gay clubs, but in straight clubs. I'd work at the door, or I would work just doing some kind of dancing, but as I said I wasn't really talented. They were basically paying me to be there. I made a lot of money, and I made my living by doing that for many years. And all of this is because of her and because she had this great taste for fashion—it had a strong impact on people. It wasn't just that we were trans, we were wearing this crazy stuff that she would make with her hands. And when the time came when I didn't have a place to live, she took me with her and I lived with her, and she helped me through many situations that weren't the happiest situations.

She showed me a lot of love. She was also a person that was dealing with a lot of issues, I guess mental health issues and things like that. But I guess that gave me a lot of understanding of what it is to live with somebody that has untreated mental health diagnosis, and how hard that is. But it showed me that it is possible to have lives around people that may be dealing with mental health diagnosis, and to have them as part of our lives, and have a normal life. It gave me a better understanding of those issues, and it was hard at times. But I guess it was so much love there and so much beauty in that relationship—and I wasn't the only one. There was a lot of trans people living with her. Not just trans people, gender variant people, and we were all living together with her.

MB What was that community like? Was there a broader network that you were part of, or a scene?

CG Well, we were part of the trans community. I always was involved in many communities at the same time. That was the most artistic part of the community, but at the same time I was part of the sex workers' community because I started doing sex work. And at the same time, I was going to school until I started to transition more and more, and the school wasn't a welcoming environment for me anymore, but I had my school friends, and I had my artist friends, and I had my sex worker friends, and I interacted in all, just difficult—

MB So, very socially connected?

CG Yes, yes. I was always very social. And again, for some reason people liked me always, so I had a lot of friends. I didn't have friends, but I knew a lot of people and I was welcome in places. I was welcome in bars and clubs where trans people weren't welcome, and they would not just welcome me, but they would give me work. To work at the door, until of course I started asking myself, why do they have me working here at the door and they don't let my friends in? And I thought, this is not okay. I lost many jobs because of that. I said, "I can't work here if you don't let my friends in, what kind of shit is this?" So, they said, "Okay, if you don't want to work here, don't." I pretend I needed the money, but I was doing sex work and I also was working in hair salons.

MB Were the other trans people you knew, did they do similar kind of jobs? Sex work, clubs, and hair salons?

CG That was what we did. That was our occupations. You were either a hair stylist, you were an artist, or you were a sex worker. I did three of those things, and I was very happy. Again, I always found ways. I was telling you as a child that I was isolated, but I found ways to be happy. Working in hair was okay. Working in clubs is hard because you find people that either adore you or hate you, so it was hard working at night also, and working as a sex worker. It is a beautiful community, but the work is very taxing though. You know, I'm a victim of sexual abuse as a child. Sex work wasn't really the best job with that kind of history, because there was a lot going on there. It was hard. I just don't want to vilify sex work, but it was hard because dealing with tricks and police and other sex workers sometimes. It's not easy. It has its beauty though. But it wasn't the easiest job to have.

MB What city was this again?

CG Rosario, Argentina. It's a big city. Think of it as something like Chicago—if you needed to do a comparison. When I finished high school, I moved there in 1989 until I came to the United States in 1999.

MB So, you were doing sex work, you were doing some hair styling, some club stuff.

CG Yeah, it was my life, and I was doing a lot of drugs. A lot of drugs. I did what she told me, and I kept that.

MB You didn't die young though.

CG Yeah, I didn't die young. Well, I see I can die today, but I never thought I would make it to age 45. I always thought, 32. 32 is a good age.

MB 32 is a good age. Jesus lived to 32.

CG In a very ageist kind of way, I didn't want to be old. I never saw an old trans woman.

MB How old were the trans women you knew?

CG Now I know older trans people and trans women, but at the time nobody was older than 40. And we always look at them as oh, those old hos, right? Again, as she told me, you're going to be a whore, you're going to get high, and you're going to die young. And everything was like that. I was a whore, I was getting high, and I didn't know people older than 40, trans women older than 40, so I thought this is what it is. In my mind I was going to live until age 32 or 35 at the most.

MB What kind of drugs did you do?

CG All of them. In Argentina, I did cocaine. Just cocaine. But I did a lot of it. Lots. Tons and tons of cocaine. It became my natural state, if I wasn't sleeping. I was high on coke for many, many, many years.

MB What were relationships like for you and other trans women with non-trans women in the same jobs, in sex work and hair dressing?

CG Um—

MB When you say the sex work community, were you in a community of both non-trans and trans women?

CG No, no, no.

MB So, it's really centered around trans sex work.

CG We were trans sex workers, and very isolated. It was a lot, there was a couple of cisgender women that were extremely open-minded and trans friendly. But at the time it wasn't like sex workers were united, and it's cis and trans. We had trans zones and cis zones, without the terminology. At the time we used wording that real woman, and transvestites. We use the word transvestite and it's not derogatory in my country. Trans people, transgender women call themselves transvestite. I'm very aware that here in the United States that's not what it is, but for us it's not an issue with that word, so I feel the need to say it.

MB Would people medically transition?

CG Yes. Some people did medically transition, and we would do hormones from the black market. I don't know how people got hormones, but you'd just go and just buy hormones. But then I found out that you didn't need a prescription, you just needed to have a friend pharmacist. And they would give it to you, it was a specific plastic surgeon that would do plastic surgeries to us. I got my first plastic surgery around 21. The first one of a series of plastic—for many years I thought I found a solution for my life through plastic surgery, and I don't. I still think that plastic surgeries can be very affirming sometimes, but for a long time it was just my only way of thinking that transition could be possible. Some trans women would have SRS, and most of them would do the reassignment in Chile.

MB Would they continue working as sex workers after surgery?

CG Yes. I used to think it was funny, they wouldn't go to work with cis women. They'd still work in the trans area. I always thought, men are looking for trans sex workers because of the genitalia, right?

MB That's what I would have thought.

CG One time I asked her, "Why don't you go and work with cis women?" Again, I wasn't using this vocabulary, I was using all the vocabulary that may come across as transphobic nowadays. I don't want to repeat it, but I said, "Why don't you go work with cis women?" And she said, "No, why would I, and lose all these clients? They don't know what I have. When the time comes and to find out, they already gave me the money. If they want me to fuck them, I have dildos. If they want to fuck me, they can fuck me—I have an asshole and I have a pussy, and most of the time they don't even want that. I do more business working in the trans area," she said. And I'm like, that sounds right.

MB And you were saying that some people were more genderfluid?

CG Yeah, yeah, yeah, yeah. For many years, I didn't fully transition, I guess, and I'm quoting this. I worked in a hair salon as a very feminine boy. I was always using my birth name, which was associated with masculinity. But I was super feminine. I had long hair, and I would just wax my face or tweeze my face, I never had hair. I had little tits—hormone tits. People could see it. It wasn't just like nobody notices and says, "Oh, this man is going to come and do my hair." It was kind of an advantage for me, because I felt women could relate better with me. And then at night I would be full femme bombshell, working in a club or just working the street trying to turn a trick. For many years it was kind of genderfluid bender. I didn't do the masculine part with conviction, I did it more as a survival. But it was that kind of fluidity in there. It was fun, and I miss that. A lot. Like all this idea of femininity, I don't think it's going to be, unless I die today, but I don't think it's going to be the end of my life as clothes, as the feminine spectrum, as I was and somehow, I think that it's not the end of my gender odyssey. I think there's more to come.

MB Excellent. Were there terms to distinguish between trans women who were more gender bending or trans women who had SRS or trans women who—was it all the same word?

CG Yeah, we always knew everybody's business, and it was this idea of, "Oh, she's a real woman. She got the surgery." And all the girls that had surgeries with breast implants, they were closer to that idea of real. Then there were people like me that were, "Oh yeah, she's pretty, but she's not full-time." But I never gave a shit about it. I was always very secure about myself, and I hung out with the pretty girls and the girls that were done. And they were my friends, and they always welcomed me. It was just a community of people, and we all were together. The only problem was business, "Don't fuck with my money, I work here."

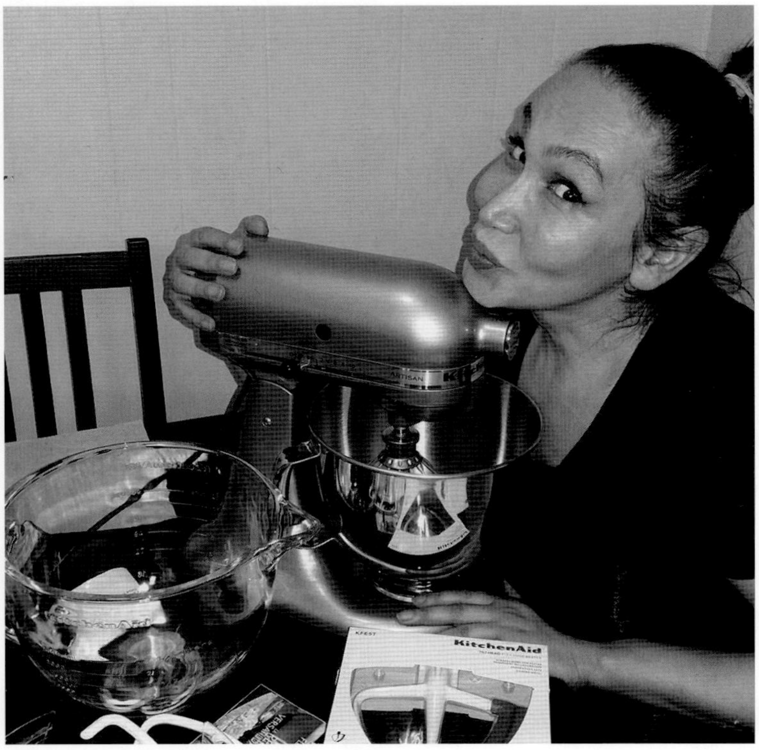
KitchenAid

MB So, real women and transvestites were the two terms that people used a lot.

CG Yes, yes, yes.

MB Interesting. Did you all engage much with social service providers or political people or religious people, like outsiders that would try to talk with you all?

CG No. It was no one outside the trans community. I was going to school, and I was kind of political, so I kind of took part and marched. I didn't think it was much of political views, it was just being part of a revolution, changing this idea of a dictatorship mentality, and what interests me. So, I did have some interactions with that.

MB With liberal or students or the left?

CG Whether it be student centers and anti-colonization. Argentina was a Spaniard colony for many years, so we have all this devotion for everything European and white. I was from the very beginning very into the rights of indigenous and the development of an Argentinian way of living that didn't have to be European. But at the same time, I was transitioning, and the idea of womanhood was the idea of a white, Nordic, European woman, right? That was the idea of what we saw as womanhood. And at the same time these conflicting feelings of, fuck the idea of beauty as it looked, when it is a white woman. And at the same time wanting to be, because that was the pressure to be. To have long, blond hair, big tits, and a big ass. Kind of, "Oh, I did these high cheekbones to look like Catherine Deneuve." At the same time I was like, "Fuck Catherine Deneuve and all the European views that conquer us." I wanted to look like her, but I hated the idea. I did things to my body to look like something that goes with an idea that I do not share, and that has its complications on its own. If that makes sense.

MB Absolutely, it definitely makes sense. Are there more stories about life in Argentina that you want to share before I ask you how you ended up moving?

CG There's many stories, but basically that's what I wanted to tell you.

MB So, you had moved to Miami and were traveling around and doing a lot of different drugs, and you were doing some online—

CG I'm not doing hair anymore; I'm not doing shows and clubs anymore. Just sex work.

MB And getting online contacts?

CG Yeah. And I'm in a relationship with this man who had a wife.

MB And you felt in love with him?

CG Yeah, I fell in love with him, and she wasn't going to take it, and she hit me in the street. She found my number, started calling me. She started sending men as clients because she knew, she saw my ad, threatening me. One time she ended up going to my house, she followed me to the supermarket and attacked me with cans of beans and celery, which is really funny. But then she did something that really scared me. She said, "I'm going to call immigration on you." And she told me, "I'm an American white woman, I can get you out of here in a minute." I remember, I sat in the steps of my apartment on 16 and Euclid in South Beach with my friend Bianca—and she said, "I love you, and I hate to tell you this, but you need to leave this place. This is not good for you. She's not going to stop—this guy doesn't love you. Go." So, she made some calls and got me a job with this girl in San Francisco to work in her house. I went to San Francisco and I started working at her house—

MB Like doing cleaning?

CG No, sex work with her. So, I go, I work with her, in her place.

MB She was a sex worker and you worked out of her home?

CG Yes, and I gave her a percentage of the money. For kind of renting the place, to live and work there. I also started going out and smoking a lot of crystal meth, and I got really scared, because crystal meth always scared me for some reason. So, I went back to Miami and I talked to my friend Bianca and I said, "I don't know, something is not right in San Francisco." And she said, "Okay, let me try with my friend in New York." She contacted her friend, and I came to New York to work here. And the first person I met in New York was Nina. I fell in love when I saw her, the first time. I couldn't think of how that can happen to me. It was totally foreign feeling of loving somebody that wasn't a man. It took me some time to understand but we started a relationship the same day. We basically went out and came back, very high on coke. We had sex, fell asleep holding each other, and we woke up the morning after, and she said, "Let's go for breakfast." I remember she wanted to hold my hand in the street—I thought that was so weird, and I didn't want it. Today, she still throws that in my face, "You fucking bitch, you didn't hold my hand in the street, I'm always going to remember that, that you were ashamed of me." I said, "I wasn't ashamed of you, it was such a foreign feeling of, what the fuck am I a lesbian now?" Questions that I even have now, but at the time it was like, am I a lesbian? Am I allowed to put myself in this category? Which today it would be like, absolutely, why am I asking this? It was 2003, 2004, and at this time the conversation was different. I'm not going to say the trans community, but the trans community that I was around, it wasn't really a thing to be a lesbian. Most of the girls were straight—how am I going to explain this to my friends, I thought. Then I remember I call my mom and I say, "Mom, I fell in love." And my mom said, "Oh my god, who is he? Is he cute?" And I said, "Well, she's actually a she." And my mom said, "What do you mean? I had a son that was gay, became a woman, and now is a fucking lesbian?" And I'm like, "Yeah, I think so." And she said, "Oh my God, you're confusing me so much." But I loved her. It wasn't a question about it. And every time I see her, the feeling is still there. In different ways. Like, we're not sexual anymore because she doesn't want to, unfortunately, but the love is there. And holding her is still one of the best feelings that I could ever have. Even now that we are not together. I loved her. I was with her for about two to three years, and we were very happy, and we were very miserable, too. I don't want her to feel guilty about it and put it on her. But she did introduce me to heroin. She didn't make me do it. I did heroin because it was another drug, and I loved drugs. But she's the one that taught me heroin. And I was not able to stop doing heroin for many years. Because of my addiction to heroin, crack, and cocaine, I wasn't the best for her. I also wasn't the best for myself. I wasn't the best for anybody. So, we broke up. When we broke up, I started seeing other people and still doing sex work. I went to my friend's house, who was renting the apartment across the hall from her. I had an apartment on fucking Mott Street, a very expensive place to live in.

MB What neighborhood was that?

CG Nolita. I started dating people and I was dating this guy, and also was seeing this cis girl. Just sexually. And this guy found out and burnt my apartment down. I came back to my apartment, and it was a yellow thing on the door, and the apartment wasn't habitable. And I was doing drugs very, very hard. I basically became homeless. I was just going from city to city doing sex work and having to find drugs in cities that are not yours is very problematic. Then I started staying with friends, but most of my friends didn't want to have me because I was shooting heroin, I guess, and they didn't want to deal with that. Nobody wanted to have me, and I went to Brooklyn, and I ended up living with this man that was taking the money that I was making, giving

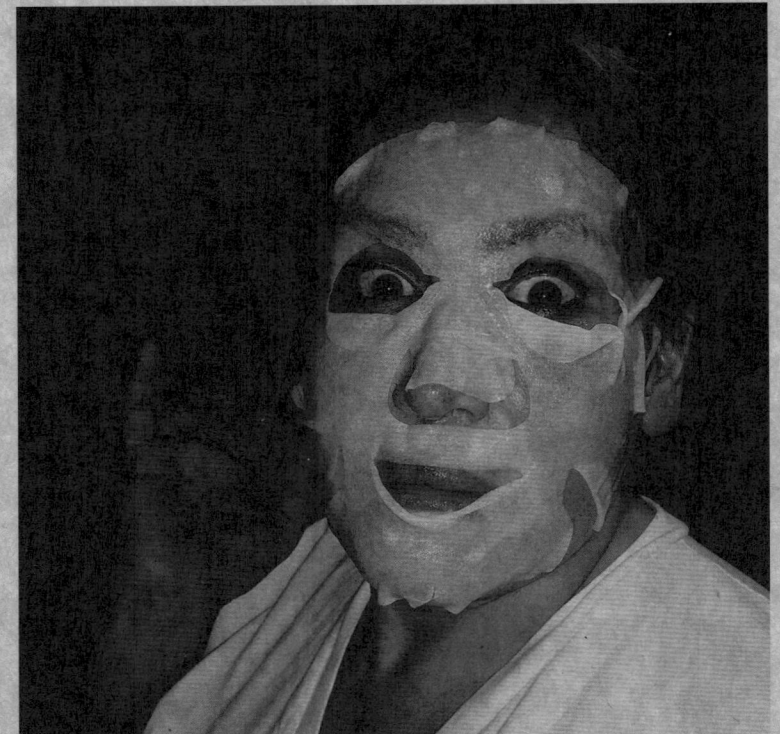

me some drugs to survive, but it was a very difficult situation, and I kept being arrested all the time. I'd be arrested for drugs most of the time, and then they would raid his house, because he would only sell drugs and have me there doing sex work, but he would sell drugs to people, like crack, and he would charge people to smoke it inside the apartment. He would get me to have sex with them and make more money. During all that process, I was also smoking crack, so I was okay, I guess. But it was a very toxic interaction. And they raid the apartment with the police.

MB Where was the apartment?

CG In Bed-Stuy—Bedford and Green. The police would raid the apartment and I'd be arrested again. One of the times that I was arrested, they just said, "You have to go to jail." So, he sentenced me I think to two months. They sent me to Rikers Island, and they put me with the men. I was detoxing from heroin, and it was horrible. Half of the men wanted to fuck me, and the other half wanted to kill me, and I wanted to die because detoxing from heroin is a very horrible, painful thing. I guess, two weeks after I was there, they called me, and the guards took me to the gym, and it was night. It was this huge gym with a very small table with a chair and a light. And it was an ICE agent, which now sometimes I ask myself, why did they give this information to ICE? Isn't it like New York doesn't do that? Why did that happen to me? It happened. The person from ICE told me that I was going to be deported, that I was going to be transferred to a deportation facility. They sent me to the immigration jail I guess here, Varick. They put me with the men, and they attacked me, and the cis women didn't want me to be with them, which is fucked up. They had to have me in isolation, which is a very, very horrible thing. And not because it was a horrible thing, but because it was expensive for them because one of those cells was supposed to have 20 people and they only had me. They let me out with an ankle bracelet, and I had to check with some kind of ICE parole officer. When I came out of there, I had to go back to that place where I was living. I was clean because my body detoxed from heroin. But I went there, and I started getting high again. The immigration officer, he went, "Why don't you get clean?" I said, "What do you mean, get clean?" He said, "Well, I'm going to send you to a hospital to do the detox." And I just did it. I didn't know what detox was. I went to the hospital, and I did seven days of detox. Then they sent me to 28 days detox. It seems people are able to, after doing drugs for so long, are able not to do drugs. So, I started contemplating the idea of recovery.

MB What was your motivation?

CG There was no motivation. It just happened. I was going to be deported. I had an ankle bracelet on all this time. From there I went to long-term treatment for 17 months, and I did it with the men, too.

MB Which program was it?

CG Samaritan Village.

MB And those are very disciplined, yes?

CG It's a horrible thing. I think that's an alternative to incarceration—it's been seven years—so, it did work and helped me face a lot of these things. They did great things for me. They got me immigration status. While I was there, I was given asylum in this country. And I came out of there and I've been clean and sober. But I also don't agree with the way that treatment is addressed.

MB Tell us about that.

CG I hate to throw the word in the middle, but I feel treatment is very patriarchal, it's very like, you are sick and I'm going to fix you. Which is the idea—

MB Like control and domination.

CG This idea of, I am right, you are wrong, and until you learn to change that, it's not space for conversation. It's not a space for debate, right? In my case, I was placed with men. And there was no space for me to say, "Let me tell you why I shouldn't be with men." It was like, you need treatment, and if you really want it, you're going to do it with the men. That is not okay with me. Somehow, it ended up working with me. But I don't agree with the way it was done. But I also have to recognize that somehow it worked with me.

MB How did they relate to your gender when you were living there?

CG I have great friends there, you know? Like my counselor is now my very good friend. And we can talk about this, and I actually met with them, and we worked on a whole policy for trans people. I feel like I made an impact there, and I'm being part of the change. Whatever they did that I disagree with, they're making their business to change. But that doesn't take away the fact that there were many things that I went through that are not okay. At Samaritan Village you have an orientation part. And then from orientation, you go to main treatment, and in main treatment you have kind of steps. It's kind of tiers. First tier, second tier, third tier, and then it's the last part when you will go and walk outside, and you come back just to sleep there. So, when I got there, I was in orientation and I was put with the women, and very weirdly nobody spooked me, because I never pass. I think it will be one in 1,000 times that I pass. I don't pass. I really don't care about passing. I know for many other people that affects them—it doesn't affect me. And I'm very clear that most of the time I don't pass. That's one of the cases where I passed. I was with the women, and nobody knew, and I had a fucking big mouth and I told somebody. I was worried that having a body that includes a penis—it's hard to hide.

MB That they would retaliate or find out.

CG And it's hard to hide, right? All the women shower together.

MB There's not a lot of privacy.

CG They always sleep together in the same room. There's no privacy. So, it isn't like, I didn't want this to be found out by somebody. And I thought I should say it. And I did, and the woman complained. Since there was no guidance from city, state, or federal on how to work with trans people, they told me that they had to move me with the men. Which was, from the beginning, a very difficult transition because all these men that saw me at the women's, now they see me there, and it's the whole kind of revealing. We are talking about hundreds of people living under the same roof, and different reactions. And my feelings about going from the female dorm to the men's dorm, including showers—

MB It sounds humiliating.

CG It is. It is a lot of domestic lifestyle. Getting dressed was one thing in the women's side, but on the men's side, it was very uncomfortable, terrifying, and very stressing. I don't know if you know—when they talk about the idea of surrendering, I really grabbed into that idea and I surrendered. And I just thought, I surrender. If they tell me to do this, I will do it, right? And I dove into the whole fixing me part.

MB But does that include surrendering your gender?

CG It should not include, but I didn't know that. I understood surrendering as a total surrendering, everything, and let them create the new me somehow, or fix the old me.

MB And were they trying to create a man?

CG No, no. no. They were just totally not sensitive to my transness. They were actually very affirming somehow. It was funny, because I was living with men, but they would send me to women's groups. I was living with men, but I didn't get any activities for Mother's Day because their understanding is that everybody that is a mother is a cisgender woman. I was in the group, so everybody was working for Mother's Day, and I wasn't. I was with the men. But I was living with them, so very, very weird. The process was wrong. And it wasn't intentional from them. I don't want to put them as the villains here. There was just no guidance. They didn't know what to do with me. They just did what they thought was best. Also, I think these places are terrified of lawsuits and things like that, and I think that for them I was some kind of liability. But they were also doing some charity with me because I didn't even have Medicaid. I was undocumented. So, nobody was paying for me, and those places live from your benefits basically. And I didn't have any benefits. Nobody was paying for me. I was going through all that with this extreme gratitude to them, which is so weird to have so many different and counter feelings about something. Sometimes I feel like I'm jumping from I love them to I hate them, and I think I did both.

MB You mentioned that you've been working with Samaritan Village around developing a better trans policy. What do you wish they had? How do you wish they had related to you and what kind of policies have you been helping them try to implement now?

CG Well, we've been working on the older allocation of clients regarding to gender identity, and it has nothing to do with gender assigned at birth. Although they're a super straight place, people should have an opportunity to say, where I find myself in the spectrum of gender, I should be here, right? And if that is not the male or the female, they should have an area that is for people that are non-binary.

MB Oh wow, have they set that up?

CG In bathroom policy. They're working on it and creating equity. Because sometimes a trans person needs that specific extra push, right? I think I was successful because somehow, I had a case manager that understood that case management and counseling wasn't going to be enough. To be around drug counseling, it had to be an extra part about my issues around gender. And she understood that she wasn't ready to do that, and she sent me outside to get that.

MB Where did you go to get that?

CG I went to The Center, and I remember, taking my first counseling and going to this room and finding out that my counselor was going to be a trans woman.

MB Who was your counselor?

CG The wonderful Christina Herrera. In my mind, trans women were only supposed to be whores, but Christina works eight hours a day as a counselor, and not in sex work. Then she told me, "I want you to meet another group of people, some of them are sex workers, some of them are not." She took me to the group, and I remember the first group was the biggest group of trans women that I'd ever seen. I thought that was the most wonderful thing in the world, a group of trans women in the same room, 70 of them. For some reason I think they were all waiting for me. It was a big room, but it was extremely crowded. Some of them were sex workers but some of them were lawyers. And I'm like, what do you mean? They can be lawyers?

Some of them, they work at Target—and some of them would do sex work too. I have to say they're mostly white women, the ones that are the architects and lawyers and things like that. But I've never been afraid. My mom always told me, "You're not less than nobody." And when I saw all of this, I said I can be one of them. I can do other things but being a sex worker.

MB I imagine it really helped with your recovery to have that help.

CG Yeah, I can be one of them. I choose not to do sex work anymore, and I finally see another possibility. Because before in my mind, sex work was the thing that I was supposed to do. Learning that there was another choice in life and making the decision to take it has been fundamental in my recovery and my overall wellbeing. I made that decision, and soon enough they asked me if I wanted to facilitate the group. I made many mistakes. I gave many, many awful, regretful groups. I gave groups that were so binary sometimes, like talking about an idea of femininity, and some guys asked me, "What are you talking about? I don't want to be that kind of woman." But I learned. We all learned together. And then they told me, "There's an internship here if you want to do it, and it's paid."

MB Were you out of Samaritan Village at this point?

CG So, I was still living there—I started getting an internship, but I was still undocumented. While I was at Samaritan Village, they connected me with a lawyer from Catholic Charities who did my asylum. So, I'm at Samaritan Village, being in recovery, connected to all this trans paraphernalia. And getting with an asylum process. Part of the whole trans thing was me doing an internship. That was a paid internship. But I wasn't able to get paid because I didn't have a Social Security number. It's very funny, the day that I got my work permit, that was about the same time when my internship was going to finish. I went to The Center, and I told them, I got my work permit, and they said, "If you go and complete this paper right now, we're going to be able to pay you retroactively for the whole year's internship," and that's how I got the money to get out of treatment and rent a room.

MB Because it was enough to put the deposit down.

CG Everything worked so perfectly. And when I was doing the internship, this amazing person named Ady Ben-Israel asked me to do a resume, and I said, "What am I going to put in it?" And Ady said, "You know, things that you did in your past." And I said, "I can't put that I did sex work," and Ady said, "You can say that you were an entertainer." Ady helped me change the vocabulary for years of work without saying what work it was. Ady explained to me that sex work has, like a big part of—how do you, customer—

MB Relations or satisfaction.

CG Relations, satisfaction, so Ady helped me phrase all of that and create a resume. And with that resume, I applied for a job at Apicha as a Patient Navigator. And I had a job, and I was able to do everything wonderfully, right? I got everything on time, and six months later, Apicha advertised the position for a Trans Clinic Coordinator—the trans clinic was very new at Apicha. My friend who worked here then, we became very good friends at Apicha, he came in and he said, "Why don't you apply?" And I said, "Because they're asking for a bachelor's degree." And he said, "I'm a good writer. Let's sit together and write something explaining why they should hire you without a bachelor's degree."

MB Like a cover letter.

CG Yeah, a cover letter. When he said, "You know, because I don't have a bachelor's degree doesn't mean that you shouldn't give me this job because I can do it. I can do it, and this is why you should hire me." And they hired me. And I will forever be grateful to Dan because he's been one of the most empowering people for, like, a white, cisgender straight dude. I would never expect that. And he was super empowering. And I got the position and when I left Apicha, they had 625 patients. So, I grew the shit out of that place. I worked there for four years. Then I kind of got tired of doing direct services and got the opportunity to come here to the pol department. That came about and I took it, and I've been here at GMHC for one year. It's been one year that I've worked here doing policy and public affairs.

MB That's incredible. In my job—I work in AIDS services—I would see a lot of trans women of color who would go in and out of peer educator kind of positions, and then another layer of trans women, mostly white, who had social work degrees sort of doing some administrative jobs. And very few people like yourself that worked as peer educators who spent time on the streets and then moved into a position of administration and authority and real influence.

CG Thank you. I mean, I don't think I've got real influence, but thank you, that's very nice to say. I don't want to come across as with an idea of success for the community, because success means different things for everybody. When I meet this girl that is where I was seven years ago, I don't even want her to go where I went. I want her to go where she goes. She wants to go right, so—I don't want to come across as like, oh, successful, I was able to get out of sex work and now as an advocate— in my book, my personal idea of success is what I wanted. So, I am successful. Other people may find ideas of success that are different, but for me it is where I wanted to go and how I defined success was to be here. Like, to have a fucking office where I can close the door and do this fucking interview with you, and nobody bothers me? It may sound mundane and stupid, but that was part of my idea of success, and getting this office was huge for me.

MB You have a door you can shut.

CG Yeah, I have a door that I can shut, look at this. I'm going to open it, look how it sounds.

The full transcription and audio file can be found here:
https://nyctransoralhistory.org/interview/002-interview-of-cecilia-gentili/

Sands Murray-Wassink

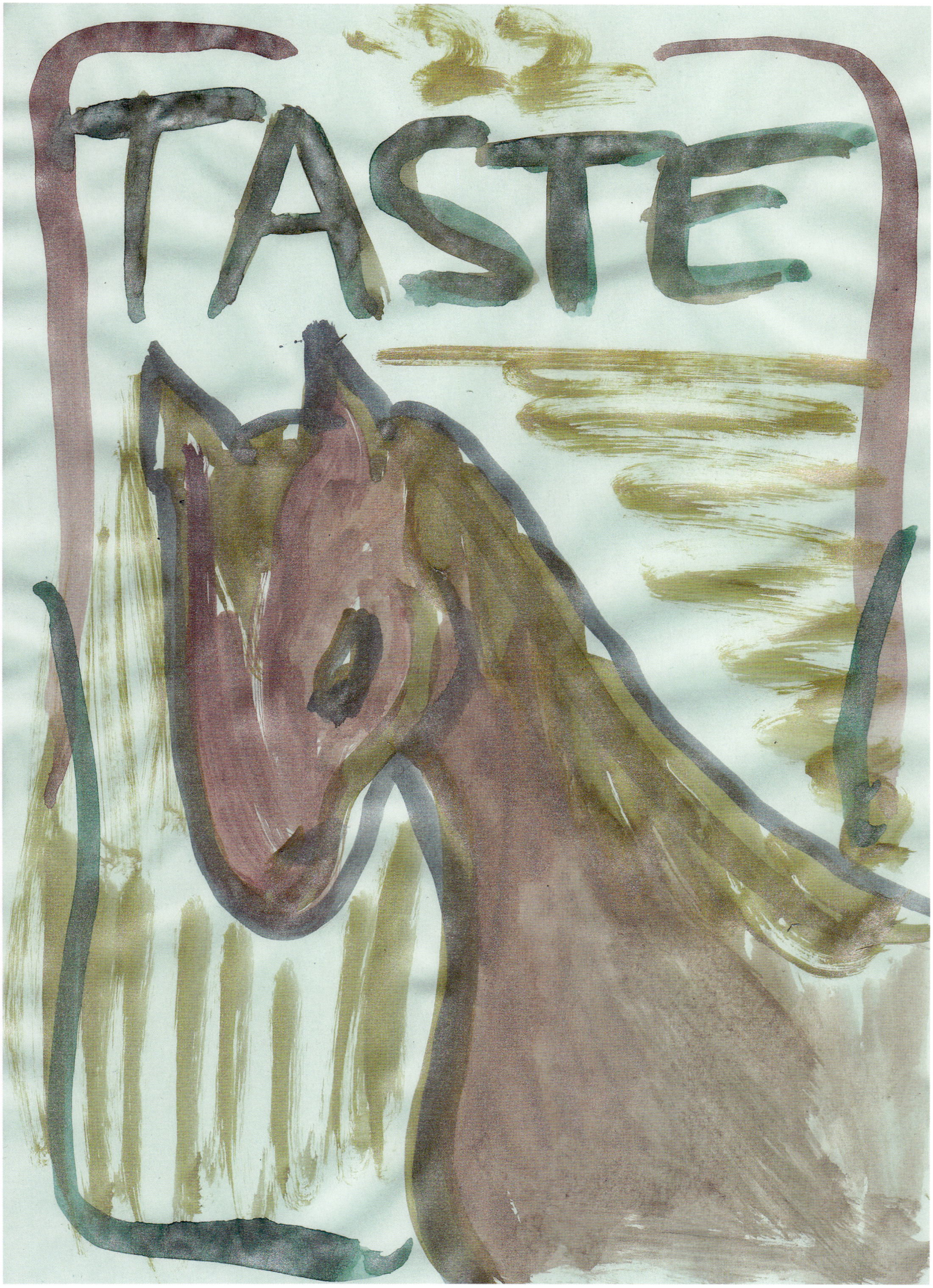
TASTE

Fear

Penny Goring

I fear there is no god.
I know there is no god. I fear this.
I fear I have no faith. I fear death.
I fear love.
I fear responsibility.
I fear there is no one person I could love completely and for ever. I fear myself.
I fear my body and brain.
I fear my addictive nature and the way it tricks me. I fear my mood swings and instability.
I fear money. I fear poverty.
I fear my anger. I fear ageing.
I fear fat.
I fear food.
I fear relapse.
I fear my perversity. I fear my sexuality.
I fear I will not get what I fear I want. I fear what I want.
I fear I will not get what I need, let alone want. I fear lonely, drunken, drugged-up defeat.
I fear arthritis.
I fear hip replacement.
I fear ugliness and stupidity. I fear violence.
I fear war.
I fucky hate it when I can't get through to you. I fear people.
I fear outer space
and the Ku Klux Klan and the gas chambers
and murder and rape and Vikings on horseback who will slash my spine and pull out my lungs to make the sign of the eagle.

Marie's Story

Claire DeVoogd

It is said God has built a simple machine in the center of the ocean. The ideas and colors get processed through it, making time into different molecules factory angels measure finding patterns that tell stories. These stories are things that happen and things that don't. Man invented fiction at the same time as revolution and himself. Reading doesn't make words, the word is a machine for making reading, magical to the degree that any machine may be. Could you but see the aspects working all together there where the machine scythes and churns the sunken earth so breathing is invented, you'd become a prophet, and mad, for you cannot tell these things but by that stupefying gap between a metaphor and the array, like blossoms, of their inevitable historicity. These belong to one another. They are in love. Sugar was consecrated to fuel primitive accumulation. Sugar sweetens the pact. It explodes. The walls of federal buildings marble canvases for violent sentiments in purple, brown: immediate, absolute, seen. Necessity grows clearer, a glass flower it's almost ready for.

They want an explosion they describe like an insatiable baby to swallow the earth, to enter reality, which is hell. They hate and fear the old gods because the old gods belonged to people they obliterated who if they came back would destroy them, being huge and disobedient to the order of things as they are today, hating them for having killed them, for being those for whom they deserved to die. It's a blessing those people died that we profit, they say, and live today as masters of it, this hell, which is systematic, and the system of it a way to know hell. To kill a people is to kill a god. To erect statuary. To turn it to gravel. The old fountain cracked in half with its ancient grammar rubbing away stands in a bus terminal and the poor lie in its shade, among grackles gleaming and leaping in car exhaust. Others have lunch. In this way it grows more and more lifelike.

A people of four may make a community and set about becoming a system to distribute power. The coffee, the dishes, the sofa, the insects and little ecocide in the kitchen; the illness, alcohol, silence, books and paintings and playlist are signs to distribute power. This is a lesson. Anything can be. The corn grown in lines and clusters with its big unnatural seeds renamed the English word for grain is harvested. Another of God's years starts. The corn sleeps in silos in the silent cold time.

When the ocean tries to take you, yell its name, loud. Using the strength of your legs and lungs come back to land. That seed is not for you, not tonight. So I sleep in a church tonight. The waxen yellow in the wings. There are words inside everyone and sometimes they are coming out still green a fruiting bush. Wed in an alley. Where the wedding isn't so loud in the alley we can gather and speak, where the weeds seed and split on air, leap where wind goes. So I sleep in a church tonight, so what if I sleep in a church. So I am weeping, so what. There are houses and the bodies of dead men down here in oak and bronze. Can the trees be ok barely moving in a little watery wind as if their tongues had been taken out. Above the hurricane is leaping across the waves it will soon break on green land and shatter things. Gemlike the water will jump from the ocean, the great fish will come rolling out with their mouths clapping. It will damage you, take your heart, take your tongue which might be a vine growing out of your heart wrapped around it, a bindweed.

Mulberry purple the ice eddies in, up and down. Black of ink, which is reddish black. And the tomatoes splitting, a tea, red ice and eyes of fish you suck out, and their red eggs in the little spoon in February. We are always waiting in February for something to happen. Then it's March, and everyone breaking up. It's fucking cold on Easter Sunday for ballet practice in the yard. Then everything is broken up. April covers the house in pain, alexandrine, cayenne, ochre, coral. And feathers, the feathers are coming out becoming nests for parrots' eggs. They all know how to read. Everyone does, thinking in the plaint language forms and shades about the millions of things they see each day, everyone does, even the dead do. Their language is sad in its utility, not right away but afterwards. Its afterthought is sad and red and buried beneath the lindens. The parrots' feathers all come up in rows like carrots grasped by the greens between knuckles and heaved, shaken, dipped, sunset, cropped, marked, shaped by a memory of soil, grave rubbings. These fish are coming up in huge nets all fallen together and shuddering, gasping, dying silver. Everything is coming up. The nets seek to go lower, to scrape the soft palate. They think there's nothing to do but scrape. Everything gets poured out and breaks up. The cement is cracking. There's nothing to do but the airport today, tomorrow something else at the airport, something violent.

At night I live in a garret next to a human animal that eats carrion, human carrion. I live over industry. He eats over it. I stay in at night. As long as he isn't hungry and doesn't see me I will be all right. He's pale as apple flesh, long, quiet because he has no language. He can't read. He breathes and doesn't hate me. He knows I am there, he leaves me alone. There are other things to eat. But the flood is coming and the tornado. A great storm is coming and things will change. I'll have to go out. I tell you to be quiet. We'll wait as long as we can.

Yesterday morning the bee starved for the basil, white beads and chalices it touches and pulls away to seem a sorcery the air holds up. How it thinks by hanging itself in the body of air, strange, everything is strange in morning yesterday. Green things with the sheen on them of virgin times. A moss so green it bleeds real blood. A missile range of morning glory in the minefield. Starved leaves come on small as vapor drops and russet mouths between are biting, stinging, growing skins. Inside me there is nothing but gardens. Endless ones, covered in string of pearl, in paintbrush. Material culture lasts a long time in pigment, vellum, rope, ink, glaze. Half-life of silicon 170 years. The matter of our knowledge tells us things, what the future is, what we are thinking it is, what we are thinking, what we are thinking it for.

Early this millennium I grow terrified and weep in the gas tank, to know, in my bowl, the kind of meaning I will be, the million molecules of breath coming to sex, insect, putrescine, cadaverine.

At evening I eat soil from a little spoon. I extend my tongue carefully to taste it and it moves there in a thousand inconsistencies of miniscule and sugar. I take it into me, devourer. The sunset is two thousand variations, all feelings becoming indigo, and the Perseids are falling, drenching, blue stains. One taps on a hill and it lights up orange, a parrot's wing fixed to a shoulder coming down. Kicking there, kicking up and down the shoulder from putrefaction into opening and black while all the words for things are spoken.

This torch is a hard thing like a cyst or pearl in the breast, the arm, that origin the liver is, not a line of credit, not something you carry. You only know it sometimes, but it's there. Suddenly it's something you feel, a cut, then a canyon, seeming illusion in the strange and dreadful verticals covered in wing-like striation and earthly fluids. No one goes in there, not to that river, not to drink. Then it's not there and it goes away again. Day starts.

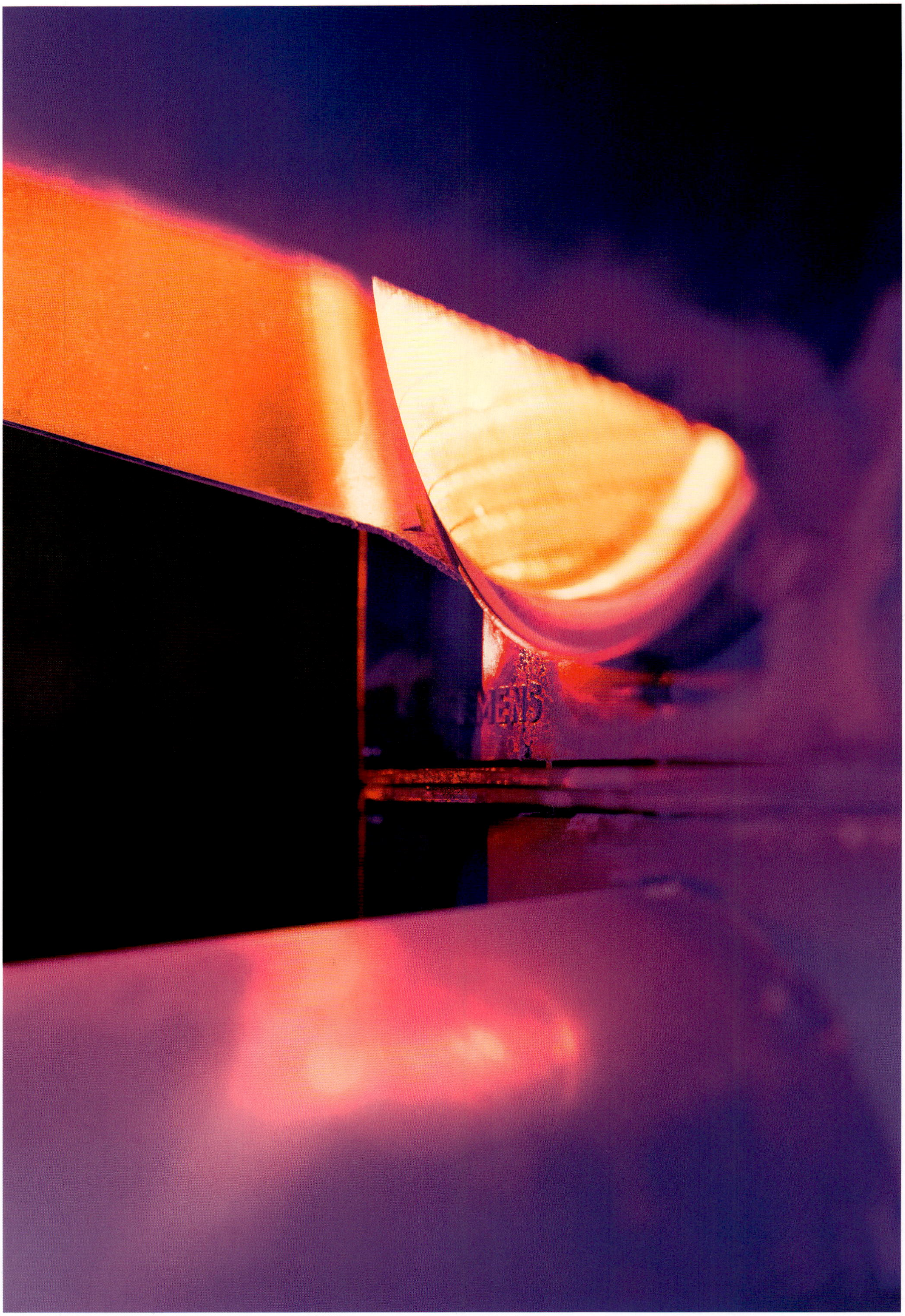

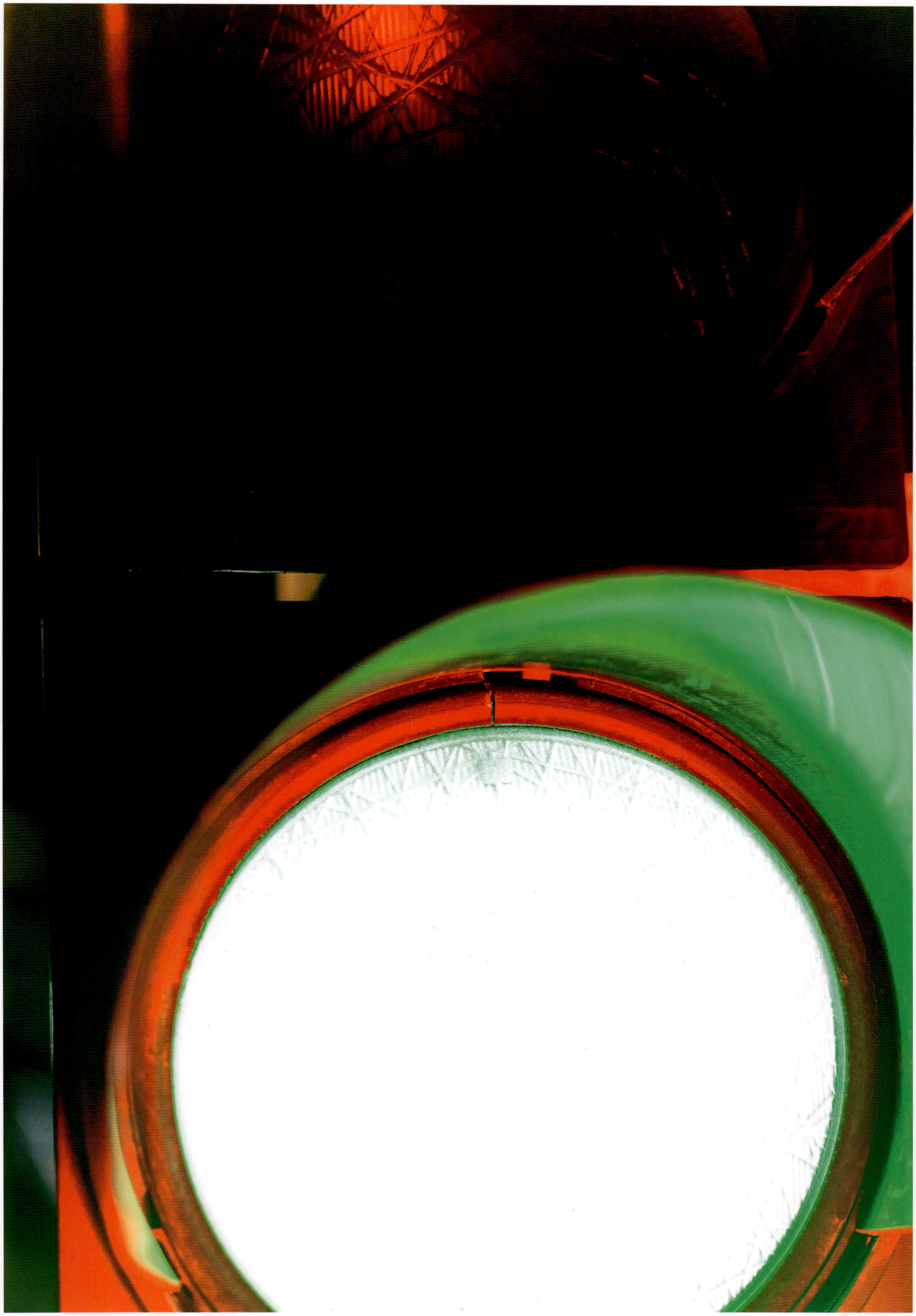

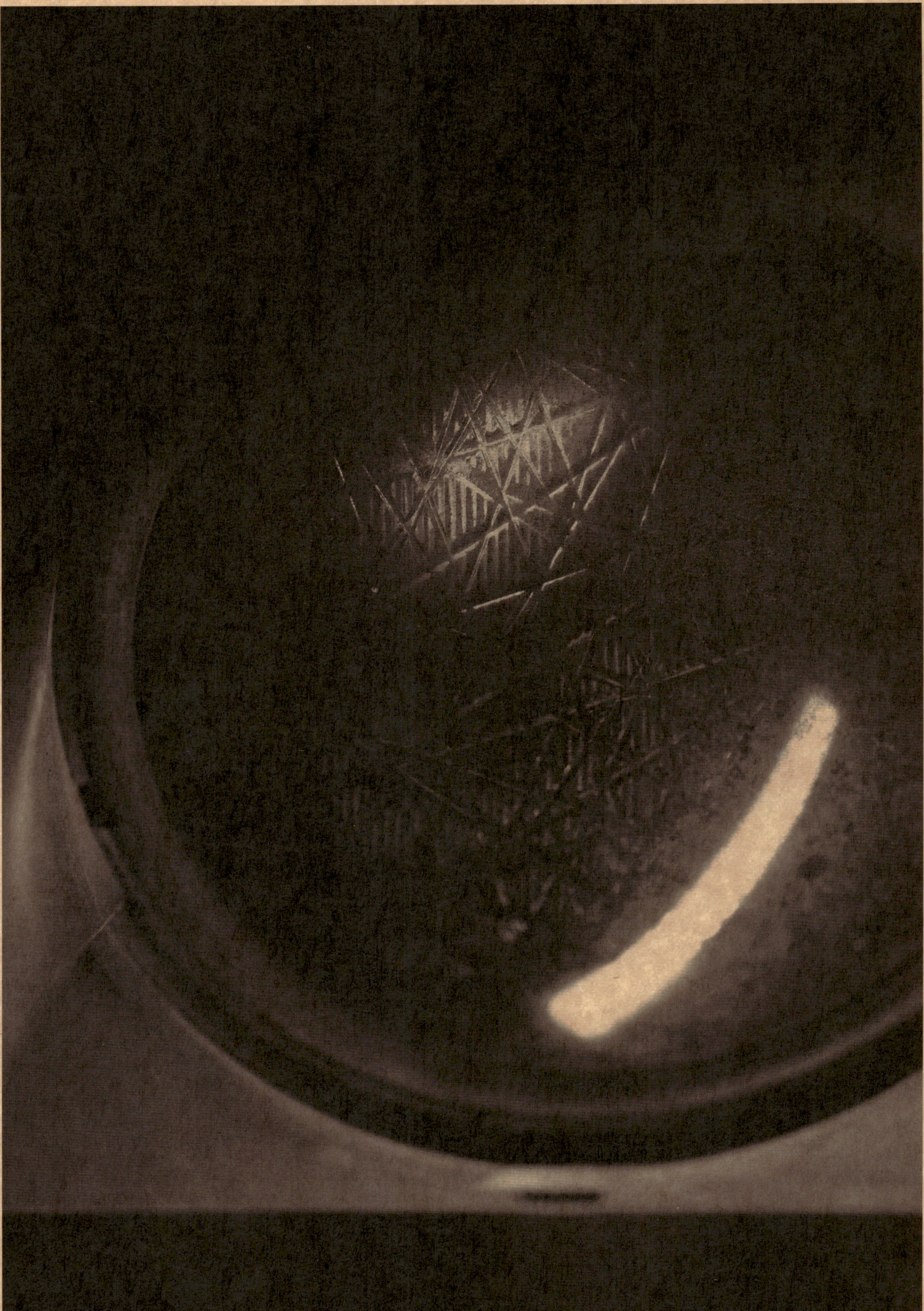

Up There and Down There: On the Low and High Levels of Drugs

Anja Dietmann (AD), Jakob Tanner (JT)

In this interview, Pfeil editor Anja Dietmann and historian Jakob Tanner discuss what exactly it means to be high, and explore how the use of drugs has changed over time. Additionally, they discuss legalization, prohibition. and the classification of intoxicants and psychedelics, as well as the motives for their consumption in a modern society.

AD Thank you so much for taking the time to conduct this interview with us. Could you introduce yourself to our readers?

JT I am a historian and a professor at the University of Zurich. I have been an emeritus since 2015 and still see myself as an expert on societal change who does not take things for granted but strives to historicize them. I have been studying Switzerland's entanglements with National Socialism since my undergraduate days and wrote a dissertation on the topic. Between 1996 and 2001, I was a member of the Independent Commission of Experts Switzerland-Second World War, which had published two dozen studies on various aspects of this challenging subject. To this day, I continue to do research in this field. My interest in drug history stems from three sources. First, the manufacturing of heroin, morphine, cocaine, and other alkaloids was highly important to the Basel pharmaceutical industry in the decades after 1900 and thus part of Swiss economic and corporate history. Second, the use of drugs is closely intertwined with the norms of society and everyday practices, with people's self-images, modes of appropriation, and forms of subjectivation. I published widely on the history of food and eating habits and have considered drugs as an integral part of these practices. In addition, there is a panoply of mind-altering substances. Their use reveals that social norms are behavioral expectations and that drug-induced deviations are often reacted to in negative, repressive, exclusionary and disproportionate ways. Third, drugs can be analyzed from the perspective of the history of the body, medicine, psychiatry, and scientific research, which opens a wide range of questions. Thus, I always choose a multi-faceted approach that attempts to blend different dimensions of what drugs can be and have been. My personal experiences in drug use are rather poor. So, I do not write from an individual concern, but I work as professional historians do, using a large number of historical sources from a variety of archives that reveal how drugs were produced, distributed, consumed, socially constructed, culturally evaluated, idolized, and demonized. It has always been crucial for me to communicate my research findings to the wider public and intervene in the debates about drug policy, thereby expressing a forthright criticism of the failed drug-prohibition regimes of the long 20th century.

AD The term *drug* can refer to both medicine, and at the same time, to intoxicants. Can you tell us more about their historical connection and diversion? For instance, I'm thinking of the shift from heroin and opium as readily available narcotics in every pharmacy—to illegal drugs. Or what we are seeing today with the progressive decriminalisation of cannabis, that started with its legalization for medical purposes.

JT The Greek word narcotic means both cure and poison. Paracelsus, a 16th century scholar, came up with the view that toxicity depends on the dose. As long as remedies were taken from the natural environment, people depended on the rich traditions and knowledge of the healing capacities of plants and organisms. Opium was considered "God's own medicine" and was indispensable as a painkiller and a remedy against diarrhea. In 1805, a German pharmacist crystallized for the first time an alkaloid from raw opium, which he named morphine—after the Greek god of sleep. The industrialization of the production of derivative drugs began in the 1830s. An increasing number of alkaloids were discovered, and in 1859 cocaine, the active ingredient of coca leaves, was successfully extracted in a pure form. In 1898, the German pharmaceutical company Bayer launched Heroin and Aspirin at the same time, in accordance with their motto, "We always have something new!"
Most of these novelties required a doctor's prescription, but this was easy to obtain, so sales of these drugs grew strongly. Bayer long ignored early warnings that heroin—a morphine derivative—was highly addictive. The International Opium Conventions of 1912 banned these substances. However, many countries took their time ratifying this treaty, i.e., implementing it on their territory. In 1925, cannabis was also added to the list of internationally banned substances. After 1933, a massive campaign was waged in the U.S. against marijuana, which was portrayed as *killer weed* and *devil's stuff*. The reasons for and effects of this prohibition policy are complex. What is consistently striking is that banning drugs has always stigmatized and discriminated certain groups of users at the bottom of the social pyramid that did not wield much power. In the U.S., since the late 19th century the suppression of smoked opium has been directed against Chinese migrant workers who were seen as cheap labor market competitors and fought as a "yellow peril." Bans on magic mushrooms (psilocybin) and cacti (peyote/mescalin) were directed against indigenous people. The campaign against cannabis increased the vulnerability of Afro-Americans and Hispanic populations, and so on. With the decriminalization of drugs, this pressure can be mitigated which in turn allows for a rational discussion about the benefits, hazards, and threats of certain drugs. It is obvious that cannabis and psilocybin have untapped medical healing potentials that have been rendered invisible by repressive policies.

AD According to your expertise, how would you define *high*?

JT *High* is the ultimate kick, an irresistible thrill. In first person documents we find many descriptions of hovering over everything that can bother, distress, and trouble you, giving the consumers of drugs an exhilarating overview. High has an illusionary capacity: it seems to unlock your best qualities and makes all the shadows and imperfections of life disappear. Psychedilia (especially LSD) can open the "doors of perception" (Aldous Huxley) in a liberating way. But anyone who throws in opiates or cocaine must know that the high-flying rush is followed by the depressing cafard. The problem is that as long as one is flying high in an "artificial paradise" (Baudelaire) one completely forgets that there is always a hard landing ahead that shatters the beautiful sensation. But the history of drugs is hardly understood without an adequate insight in the power of the *craving*.
In his seminal text *Civilization and Its Discontents*, Sigmund Freud wrote (nearly a century ago in 1928): "The service rendered by intoxicating drugs in the struggle for happiness and in keeping misery at bay is so highly prized as a benefit that individuals and peoples alike have given them an established place in the economics of their libido." Drugs are not only "drowner of cares allowing an "immediate yield of pleasure," but they offer "a greatly desired degree of independence from the external world." "Independence" means, in a certain sense,

the suspension of the law of gravity, the capability to elevate oneself above all things. This is the meaning of *high*.

It is also important to realize that *high* is by definition a relative and transitory state, an intermediate stage in a dynamic up-down fluctuation. In the realm of drugs, its frequency cannot be kept stable, because the substances applied have the disastrous tendency to lose their effect with continued use, so that more and more has to be taken in a shorter and shorter interval to achieve the desired state. This so-called "tolerance increase" of drugs drives people into a vicious circle. Many authors, Freud among them, have warned against the illusory relief and flight of fancy provided by drugs. There is no coincidence that Aldous Huxley titled his famous 1956 drug essay "Heaven and Hell."

As a historian, I am interested moreover in a much broader definition of *high*. There is a new interest in the high-low dimension in general. Attention is focused on social injustice, on the income-wealth gap that allows those *up there* to live a good life at the expense of those *down there*. A history of vertical entanglements is also what the concept of the Anthropocene is striving for. The inscription of humanity into the geology of the planet runs through the material transformation of the earth's surface, through an ever-increasing interaction of deep and high, of underground and skyscrapers. The modern way of life is inconceivable without the elevator. Drugs are, in a sense, a *lift* that transports people's mood from the bottom to the top via chemical agents. New drugs also have a connection with stock markets. For example, the current psilocybin-hype and the so-called shroom-boom promise new antidepressants with enormous sales potential. As a result, the stock prices of spin-offs in this field are going through the roof, and the deep *gold digging* of drug discovery has high flying stock prices as its correlate. *High* (in relation to *Low*) seems to me to be a very powerful analytical category whose explanatory power is far from exhausted.

AD In your article "Rauschgiftgefahr und Revolutionstrauma" you write: "Drugs are dangerous for us when we cannot integrate them into our own society, into the mass culture of a performance- and consumption-oriented industrial society." Could you elaborate more on that?

JT The war years of 1914-1918 saw a sharp increase in the use of opiates and alkaloids, and the 1919 Treaty of Versailles extended the international prohibition regime to many more countries that had lost the war, including Germany. Since Switzerland had stayed neutral, it did not have to sign the peace treaty, but came under pressure from the USA and the League of Nations. Since the major Swiss pharmaceutical companies were among the world's important producers of morphine, heroin, and cocaine, there was fierce opposition to the curtailment of this lucrative business through a prohibitive legislation. Nevertheless, Switzerland eventually had to capitulate. In 1925, a narcotics law meeting the requirement of the International Opium Convention came into force. In terms of domestic policy, this law became conceivable because the mental shock of the general strike of 1918 had triggered a penchant for normality, which was expressed in a strong aversion to intoxicants.

The social conflicts of the time turned mind-altering substances into crystallizing nuclei for anxieties. The result was a broad cross-class anti-drug-consensus. The conservatives fought for the preservation of morality, the liberal bourgeoisie wanted to secure the industrial efficiency of the working class, the social democrats and the communists (who were hostile to each other) saw in the narcotics insidious agents clouding class consciousness—and in the end everyone voted for a ban which was no longer primarily directed against the industry, but targeted drug users, who were portrayed as a danger to the normal working of society.

The role model for such an economically successful society was the USA, where the battle cry "back to normality" dominated in the early 1920s. Switzerland was in the grips of an efficiency craze. Rationalization and Taylorism were celebrated as the "new industrial religion" and America became the great paragon. In her inspiring study "Visions of Modernity," Mary Nolan pointed out that "Americanization" operated metaphorically: it was a colorful language that allowed old social problems to be reformulated in ways that now seemed solvable. The new drug discourse that became widely accepted fit well into in this regime. Drugs became synonymous with dysfunctionality. They stood for the disruption of an aspired productive social order that relied on a Fordist coupling of mass production and mass consumption, mediated by the nuclear family, which generates consumer demand and provides the labor supply.

AD Even though eventually drugs became synonymous with dysfunctionality, they still kept a prominent role in medical, behavioral, and psychological studies in the hope they could be exploited for targeted purposes. For instance, as you wrote in your text "Doors of Perception versus Mind Control," there were attempts by the USA military and the CIA to functionally re-educate people through the consumption of drugs. Can you tell us more about mind control projects, and the dichotomy between functionality and dysfunctionality with drugs? And are there other examples of the military's use of intoxicants?

JT You are right, drugs always have a variety of uses and meanings, and any attempt to fade out this diversity and inherent contradictions leads down a bogus path. It is quite simply the case that in 1923/24 there was a broad consensus in the political decision-making process in Switzerland, the common denominator of which was the view that drugs were dysfunctional for the modus operandi of a modern industrial society. The term Roaring Twenties, however, shows that this decade was also perceived as very *wild*. Female artists such as Josephine Baker stood for a breakout from convention; their dance-variétés certainly conveyed a sense of being high. This cultural exuberance, this overflowing mood, was also evident during the years of alcohol prohibition in the USA (between 1919 and 1933). It is impressively described in the 1925 novel *The Great Gatsby*. Here, F. Scott Fitzgerald renders in compelling images and scenes the decadence, debauchery, high-flying idealism, and crashing dangers of a period marked by a stock market boom, illegal drug-parties, mafia-criminality, jazz, and flappers.

With regard to the issue of the military use of drugs, a look back in time makes it clear that the deployment of drugs as *weapons* must be viewed from a dual perspective: on the one hand, an opponent is paralyzed by such agents and made incapable of fighting or willing to surrender. On the other hand, by using drugs, one's own soldiers are transformed into merciless *combat machines* that ignore risks and maximize their performance on the battlefield. A few examples of the former (all of which are well-rounded, often mythical narratives): alcohol was used as a weapon of war in the ancient world. Whoever could get the enemy drunk had a better chance of victory in a battle. As far as the early modern period (from the 15th to the 18th centuries) is concerned, the Italian historian Piero Camporesi, in his study *Il pane selvaggio (The Bread of Dreams)*, has maintained that in feudalistic societies the rebellious crowds were confused and held down by mass contamination. Particularly in times of famine, often due to prolonged rainy seasons, grain fields were infested with ergot fungus. This poisoned staple food was not thrown away but eaten because of the general hardship, so that the working classes of the population fell into a terrible state of immiseration. Camporesi's thesis is controversial—but his observation points to the fact that drugs have also been used to stabilize social hierarchies. Two examples of the latter:

in the 12th century, the Ismaili followers of the "Old Man of the Mountain" were known as assassins. Doped by cannabinol, they death-defyingly ambushed Christian crusaders during the Third Crusade. As terror zombies, they tried to spread fear and horror to prevent the conquest of Jerusalem. A modern version of this story—which took place under completely different circumstances—occurred in the 20th century during the Nazi era, when the metamphetamine Pervitin (known today as crystal meth) was used by the German Wehrmacht as a wonder weapon in the Blitzkrieg. By the end of the war, a total of 35 million of these psychic boosters, also known as Panzerschokolade, Hermann-Göring-Pills, or Stuka-Tablets, had been popped; many narratives surround bright-eyed pilots who fought daredevil battles in the skies even after days without sleep.

During the Cold War, the idea of mind control became a salient feature in the discourse about psychological warfare. As the film *The Manchurian Candidate* (1962) illustrates, drugs were not always involved. However, there were efforts to use psychotropic substances such as LSD as a combat agent. This was the case with the CIA-funded U.S. project MKULTRA, which ran in the 1950s and '60s and was shut down in 1973. Experiments with LSD were intended to show whether this drug could be applied to extract existing knowledge from humans or whether it could be helpful to break resistance. One idea was to use LSD in drinking water reservoirs or in the diets of political opponents. To what extent such plans have actually been tested is still unclear; what is proven is that test subjects have been administered LSD without their consent. Since the 1960s, drug consumption has also been seen as a vehicle for subversive warfare. Thus, the hippie and flower power movement with its slogan "Turn on, tune in, drop out" appeared as an alarming self-undermining of the youth in Western societies. It was feared that the Ostblock, as a drug supplier, was trying to weaken the foundations of the capitalist societies while itself forbidding drug use within its own ranks. These fictional scenarios reflect an ambivalent view of drugs: they fascinate not only dropouts and emancipatory movements, but also military planners and army strategists. From a military perspective, they can be weaponized and are at the same time a sneaky medium of submission; in the opposite view, they are a vehicle of liberation and self-enhancement.

AD What is the connection between legalisation, prohibition, and the consumption of drugs?

JT Legal frameworks have a massive impact on the use of drugs. They affect prices and power relations in these markets. For example, during alcohol prohibition in the U.S. (1919-1933), consumption of the incriminated beverages was cut in half, but the socio-medical and security consequences of this policy were devastating. This led to many more deaths than before, whether from poisoned drinks, gang warfare, or police violence. Loyalty to the rule of law and civil conduct within democratic society visibly deteriorated. The main winners of Prohibition were illegal producers and ruthless distribution syndicates, which corrupted the police and created a climate of violence throughout the country. The results of this policy were disastrous. Such conditions can be found in all illicit drug markets, and the "war on drugs" proclaimed by U.S. President Richard Nixon in the early 1970s made the situation even worse. Repression against narcotic substances was significantly racially biased and led to a steep increase in the African-American prison inmates. The effects of this policy marked by repression continue to have a very negative impact in the 21st century. According to new UN drug reports, about half a million people die each year as a result of drug use, and the number is rising. The reason for this is the increased potency or overdose of illegal narcotics, a lack of quality control, and a strong expansion of supply on these markets, which have also shifted heavily to the internet (digital delivery platforms).

Obviously, there are no official sales figures, but according to the UN, the turnover in the global drug business is between 300 and 400 billion USA dollars per year. The profit margins are dazzling; one is tempted to say that the desire to get high among consumers is leading to a long-term high in profits. With prohibition, the zones of illegality are growing, and organized crime is flourishing. In rural production areas and along transit routes, clashes between drug cartels are fought with brutal ferocity, and they also target small producers and civilians. Local farmer families are forced into collaboration with the drug mafia by giving them the alternative of plata o plomo (money coins or lead bullets), where the financial sums offered are exploitatively low. In Colombia and Mexico, the war against the drug cartels has resulted in hundreds of thousands of deaths and injuries since 2006. Victims are not just rival gangs, but people who can barely fight back. In some regions of the world, including Afghanistan, opium sales are used for funding terrorism.

There are studies that show that in these illegal markets, there is an asymmetric power distribution, with two poles that are almost powerless and an extremely powerful in-between. The added value-chain starts with small peasant producers at one end whose fortunes depend largely on the processing organizations. At the other end, it terminates with the drug-addicted, dependent consumers, who are pushed into procurement crime. In the middle segment, technologically well-equipped criminal organizations with state-of-the-art transportation and communications systems are able to establish a highly profitable business model whose governance is based on violence and exploitation. The organized crime enrolls in a permanent competition with the police and customs authorities. The Swiss psychiatrist Hans Kind came to the sobering conclusion that—as he put it—"organized crime and the police pursue the same interests, albeit from opposite motives." The common interest is a shortage of supply. The organized crime is in permanent competition with the police and customs authorities. By deterring and seizing illegal drugs, law enforcers want to curb drug use; criminals know that these repressive measures drive up prices. In the meanwhile, however, analysts of the drug scenes point out that the demand in the urban metropolises comes from user groups that are financially very well off and that have sufficient information about the quality of the substances.

A recent article in the Neue Zürcher Zeitung, published on February 10, 2023, states that cocaine consumers cannot ignore their responsibility: "Many of them belong to a progressive elite that pretends to understand social and ecological problems, but at the same time uses the white powder as a party drug. It's high time that consumers also become aware of what they are financing by buying the drug and how much suffering they are causing." As thoughtful as this appeal to personal responsibility is, it should not distract from the fact that the problem is not individual but structural. It is hardly possible to achieve any fundamental change in drug policy with "just say no" slogans. The real issue is the global prohibition regime as a whole, with its counterproductive effects. It is therefore necessary to focus on a political level and on international governance. Transnationally, we should move away from an approach that has now caused a great deal of harm for a whole century without solving any problems.

AD Portugal decriminalised drugs in 2001. Instead of prohibition, the state focuses more on prevention and therapy, which has led to a decrease in drug use. What do you think of this model? Could it be adopted in other countries?

JT The sole conclusion that can be drawn from my analysis of the global prohibition regime is that the model being tried out in Portugal also has a future in other countries. In Germany, for instance, the red-green-yellow traffic light coalition* is interested in the Portuguese experience. Such approaches, which focus on harm reduction, social support, and medical and psychological assistance, are currently being experimented with in several countries. In particular, the use, possession, cultivation, and sale of cannabis has been decriminalized, up to and including full legalization. Cannabis is also being released for medical purposes in various places.

Since 2008, Switzerland has been testing a so-called "four-pillar drug policy" that combines prevention, therapy, harm reduction, and repression. Syringe distribution, methadone substitution programs, and heroin prescription for addicts are available under this scheme. Under the impression of a rising number of drug deaths, the Canadian province of British Columbia has recently launched a pilot project which declares the possession of drugs up to 2.5 grams to be exempt from criminal prosecution. This is intended to provide relief for drug addicts, who are often under stress, and to allow for quality control of the substances being consumed. In many cities, facilities for drug testing at parties and festivals are allocated. Such measures have helped prevent many deaths, particularly among young people.

In this debate about legalizing, liberalizing, or decriminalizing a wide gamut of drugs, it is important to avoid a pitfall. Opponents of such steps often argue that drugs are dangerous after all and that critics of repression trivialize these dangers. This line of argument is completely misleading. As a matter of course, drugs cause problems of various kinds. They lead to addiction, some of them are physiologically disastrous, others destroy peoples' personalities. I myself remember the depressing news of the death of world-famous icons of pop music around 1970, when Jimi Hendrix, Janis Joplin, and Jim Morrison died one after the other. However, it is inconsistent to deduce from this awareness of the problems of drugs that they should be fought primarily with police repression and military methods. It is precisely these approaches that increase many of the negative aspects of drug use, and what we call the "drug problem" is primarily caused by an ideologically motivated policy of prohibition in the signum of "law & order." There are many drug-dependent individuals who know about the elusive quality of the drug-generated *high*. Yet most if not all of them do not want to be harassed and arrested by the police. They demand help, not intimidation. Decriminalizing drugs is therefore not an austerity program. Drug liberalization in the neoliberal vein will not work; such an approach produces positive results only if it is accompanied by a broad range of support services financed by communities and the state. The case of Portugal shows just that. Here, parallel to the dismantling of repression, counseling, therapy, and substitution programs as well as medical treatment have been made available. Knowledge transfer in schools, education in recreational facilities or at mass events, and laboratories that check quality on the spot are important prerequisites for a policy aiming at protecting consumers and keeping the door open for addicts to find a way back in a life beyond drug dependency.

AD   Thank you for your precious answers. What would you like to conclude with?

JT   I would like to emphasize again that the desire to be *high* and the yearning for *artificial paradises*—in their most varied forms—are powerful motives for the use of drugs in modern societies. High and low go inextricably together. So does the will to break free and the experience of constraint. There are many power techniques of staying socially *on top*; the realm of drugs, however, has an inherent risk of dropping off. The recipe for staying high is called "more of the same"—and this mode of amplification inevitably runs up against limits. Paradoxically, the prohibition regime that dominates today's global drug policy also seems to be committed to precisely this principle. When repression is not enough to make the evil being fought disappear, the policymakers call for even more police forces, which in turn only makes matters worse. In many areas of the world where drugs are produced, transferred, and consumed, this "more of the same" attitude has unleashed a depressing spiral of violence.

These experiences of violence are significantly asymmetrical, because they are targeted mainly downward, against those strata of the population and groups of people who can be described in the social hierarchy as *low*. This condition has been described in historiography with the concept of intersectionality. This explanatory model assumes a system of overlapping inequalities and attempts to understand how the simultaneous experience of socio-cultural categories (gender, race, social status, financial posture, sexual orientation) interact. It is well known that disparate forms of discrimination and deprivations related to such categories are self-reinforcing and accumulate regularly into systems of oppression and domination. In this light, today's drug policies undermine the equality premise of a democratic society. The alternative would be a more relaxed and creative approach to drugs. It will never be possible to suppress the desire for relief, for being high and having a psychedelic experience, just as the negative effects of continued drug use cannot be eradicated. These are contradictory phenomena that a democratic way of life must tolerate. Drugs are an expression of modern insecurity, and the claim that one can simply eliminate *the problem* and thus generate order and security has always been fallacious.

---

* Editor's note: In the Federal Republic of Germany, the term traffic light coalition refers to the cooperation of the three political parties SPD (red), FDP (yellow) and Bündnis'90/Die Grünen (green) to form a government majority.

Palast der Republik—Burj Khalifa

Jasmin Werner

The first time I visited the Burj Khalifa in Dubai was in May 2022, which was two years after I had already created works about it, as well as on my cousin who was living in the city. My obsession with the building had been accumulating for two years prior to my visit. It started when I found out that steel from the former GDR Palace of the Republic was recycled into the Burj Khalifa. Growing up in the newly formed German states, near Berlin, the Palace of the Republic was a known companion.

    I arrived in Dubai as an observer on a research trip, following a fanatic interest, like a stalker finally approaching its object of desire. Admittedly, during the drive from the airport to the hotel, I kept wanting to glance up to see the oversized glittering skyscraper, which was not particularly difficult to find in the night sky. The Burj Khalifa, the tallest building in the world, seems to stand out completely from its surroundings, quite out of proportion compared to the skyscrapers near it. Its beauty is questionable, though its construction is impressive. The Burj Khalifa stands on sandy terrain in a windy desert. At 826 m, it rises almost 1 km into the air.

    The next day's tour, *At the Top, Burj Khalifa*, was, as with so many tourist attractions, anti-climactic. Reaching its entrance through the Dubai Mall, the biggest mall in the world, consumerism and infotainment engulfed the nervous crowds. Most visitors scurried quickly past the exhibition, which was showcasing the complex construction and maintenance process. People were rushing to get to the lifts that go up to the 124th floor at 36 km/h. When I reached the top, I wandered around on the viewing platforms feeling somewhat lost. I browsed the souvenir shops and watched other people taking photos of their companions. No one else seemed to have the idea of going up by themselves. After all, if alone, who would capture their memory? When I tried to take a picture of myself at one of the many designated photo spots featuring angel wings hovering over the Dubai landscape, a photographer on duty took pity on me and captured me in various social media-ready angles quickly on my phone.

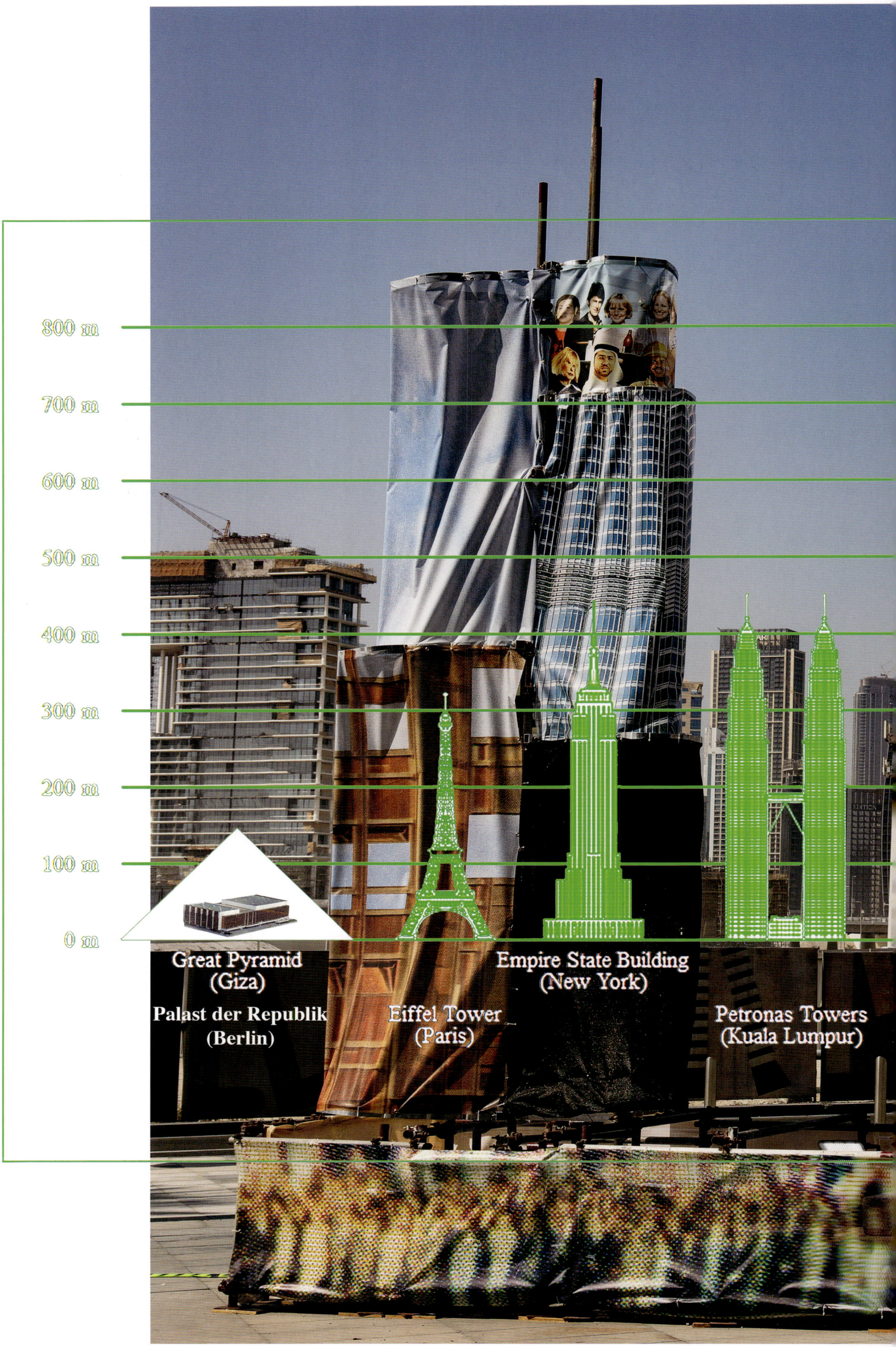

800 m
700 m
600 m
500 m
400 m
300 m
200 m
100 m
0 m
Great Pyramid (Giza)
Palast der Republik (Berlin)
Eiffel Tower (Paris)
Empire State Building (New York)
Petronas Towers (Kuala Lumpur)

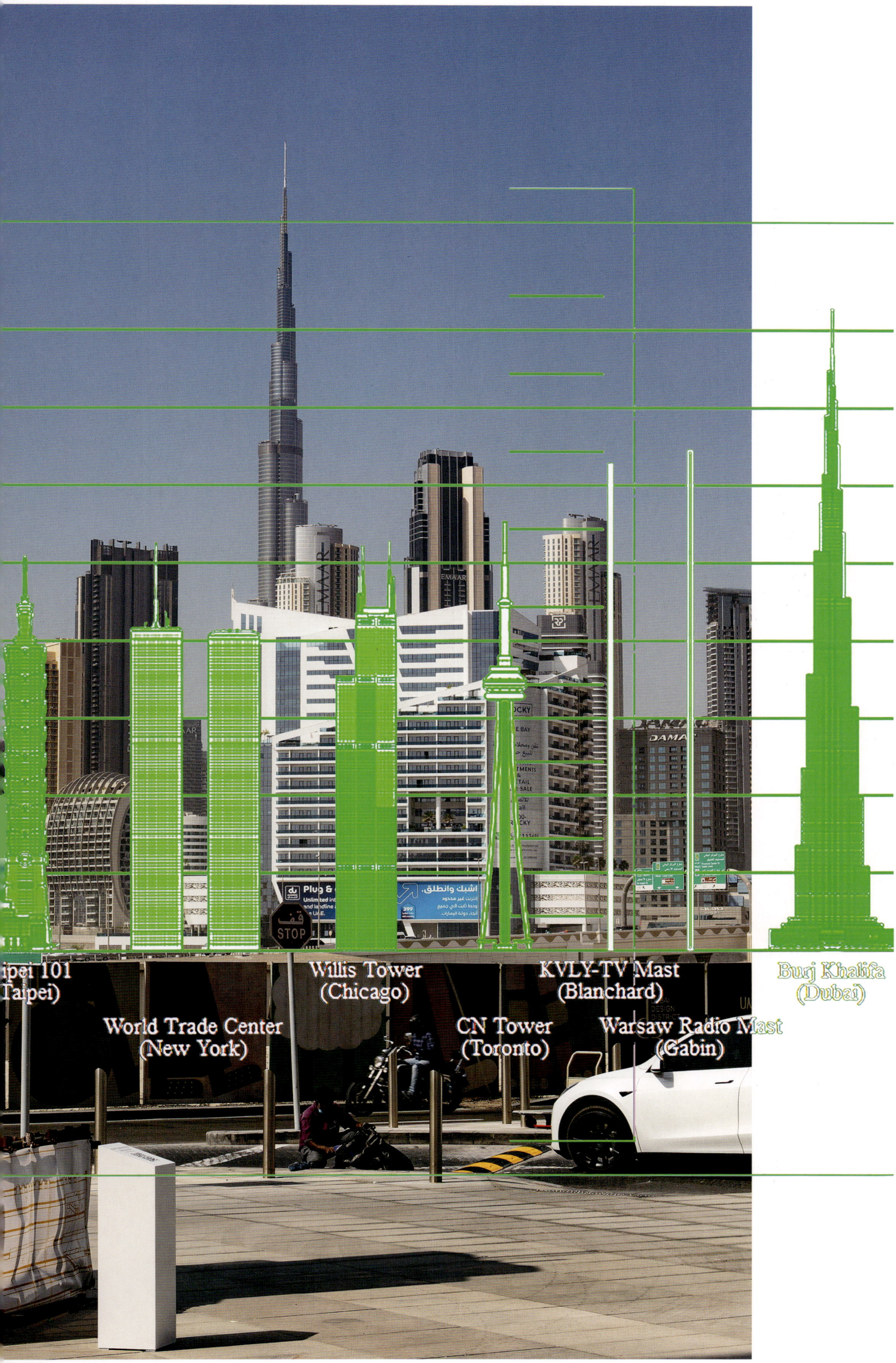
ipei 101
Taipei)
World Trade Center
(New York)
Willis Tower
(Chicago)
CN Tower
(Toronto)
KVLY-TV Mast
(Blanchard)
Warsaw Radio Mast
(Gabin)
Burj Khalifa
(Dubai)
STOP
EMAAR

The View

Jane Joritz-Nakagawa

orientalism event
crocheted brain
a slave to echolalia
so lumpy it's hopeful
blanket breath
zero bracket
coma flesh
have you eaten yet

concubine culture
yellowed houses and teeth
a whitened neck
butchered in my brain
the bump on my head
stays there forever

in my desire
a casket of fleas
warned by the wind
my hand on my heart

tedious qualifications
for an invisible ocean
rosaries and flowers
dot the matrix
tunneling my faith
in useless habits
dot dot dot

failure mounts
on top of me
pushing me sideways
like a German expressionist
disguised as a geisha
in a Japanese temple

an experimental whack
a museum out of touch
a mall out of luck
shots fire some flee

remember your body
how it flowered
i pluck the leaves
and chop the stalks

dinner time
in your head
breaks the mood
of tv broadcasts

wheezing and simmering
smiling painfully
a boat without a hull
shoes but no suitcase

the exercise
your brain gets
watching a screen
without a license

my back is
covered in moss
because it misses you

to protect it from lice
i dreamed my disability
was all in my head
a dearth of proliferations
synonyms of gadflies

longing for elevation
but my head is too punctured for that

screaming and streaming
low to the ground
a bonfire on a road
full of tripwire
hidden tragedies are
trajectories for
an exempt limb
a maverick afterthought
a mother vehicle
on an unattainable path
in an abstract field

i take out
my tortured past
on my students
who look up and smile

gracefully
impossibly
apologetically

the depths make me dizzy
the view from here ancient

Toad Retreat

Gerrit Frohne-Brinkmann

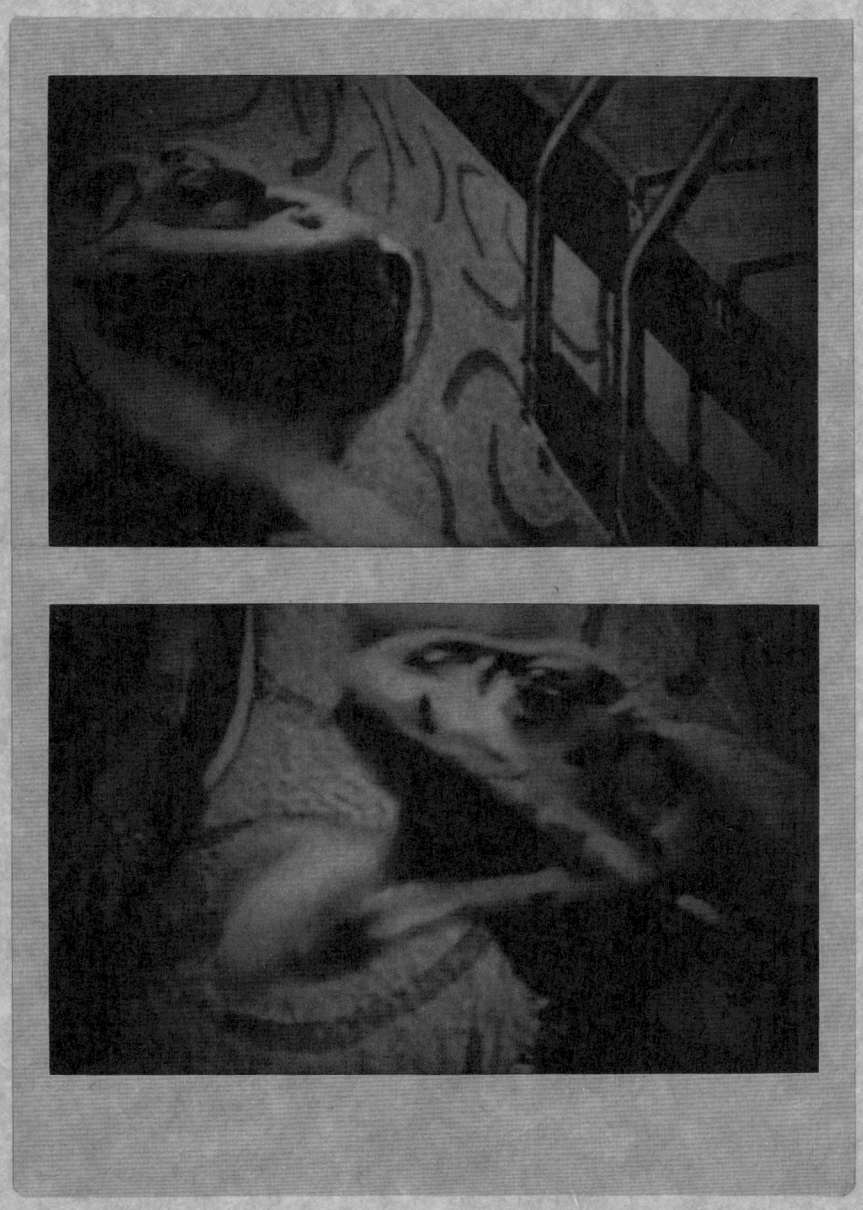

31

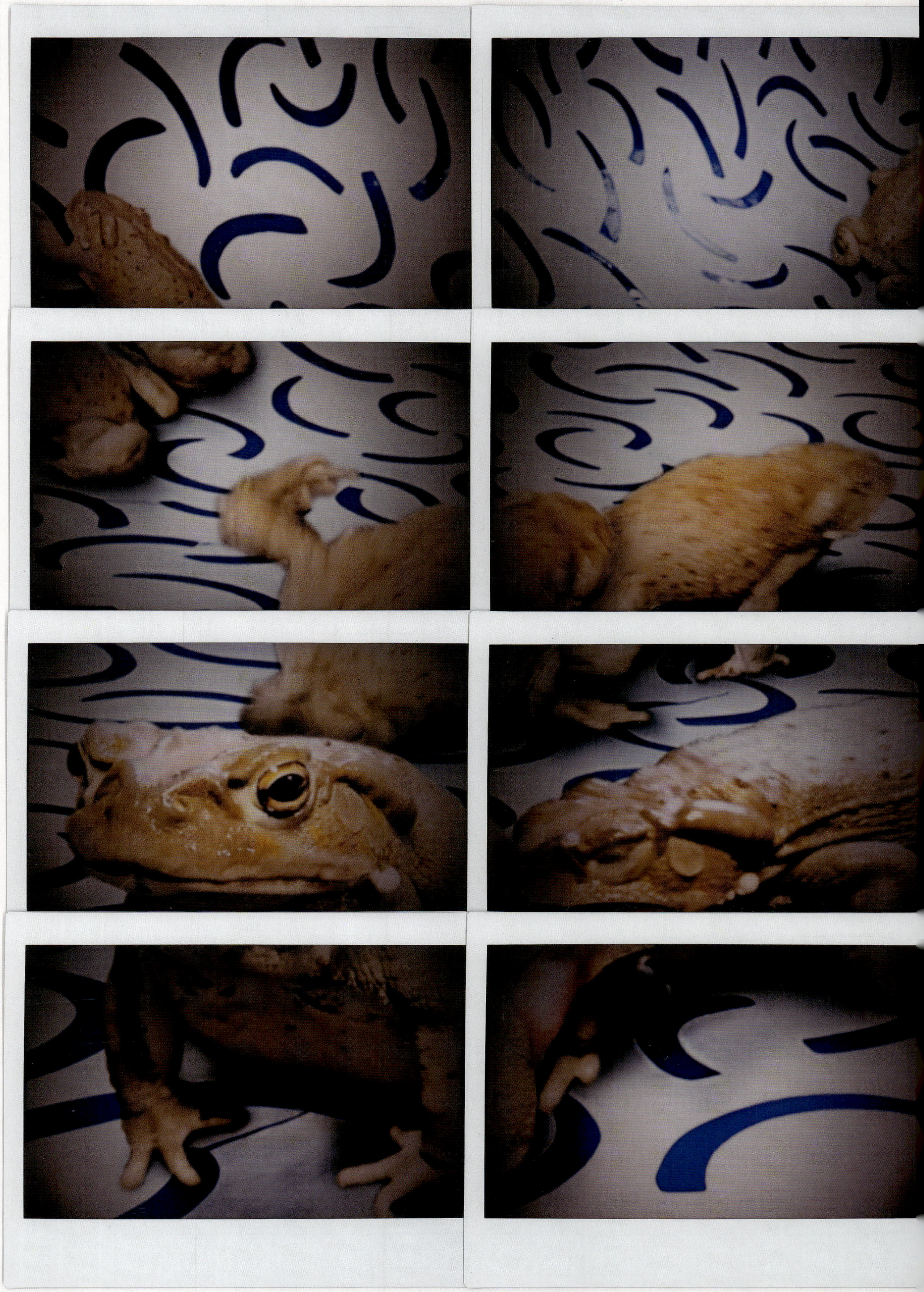

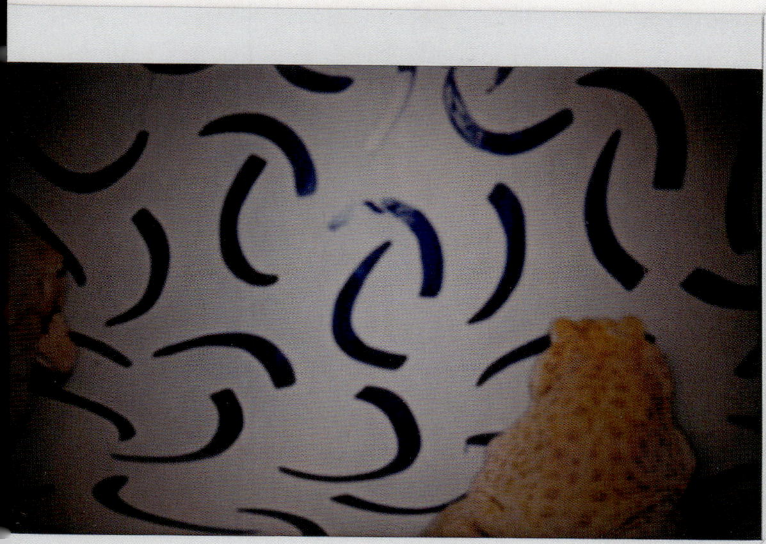
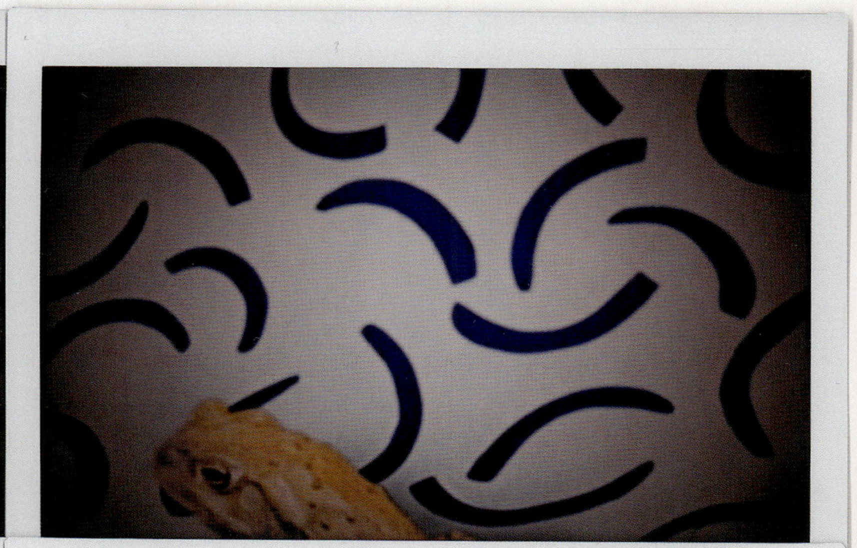
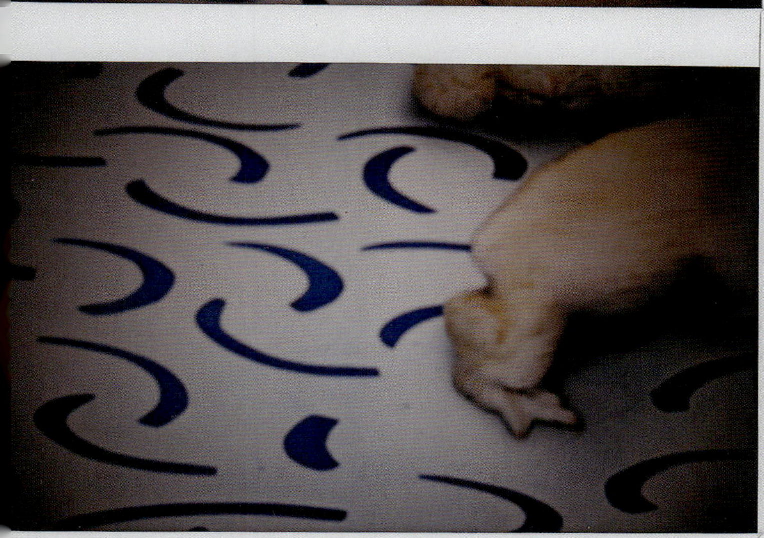
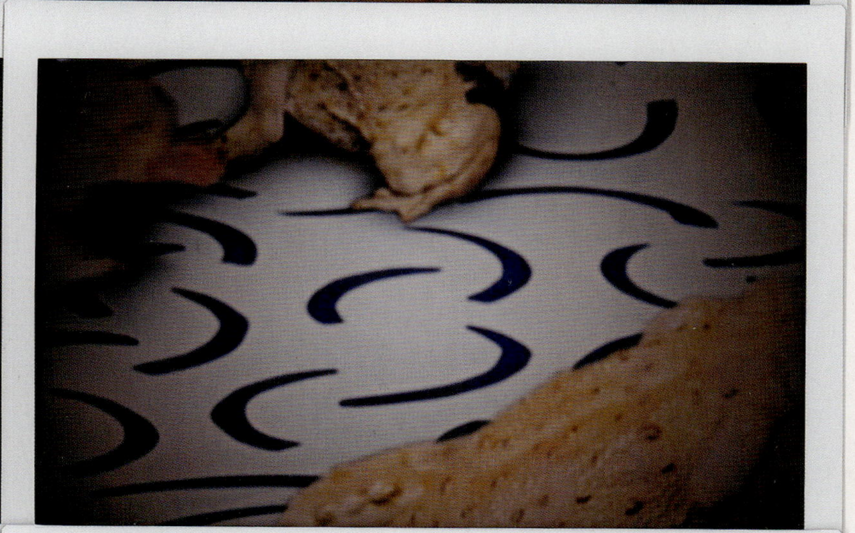
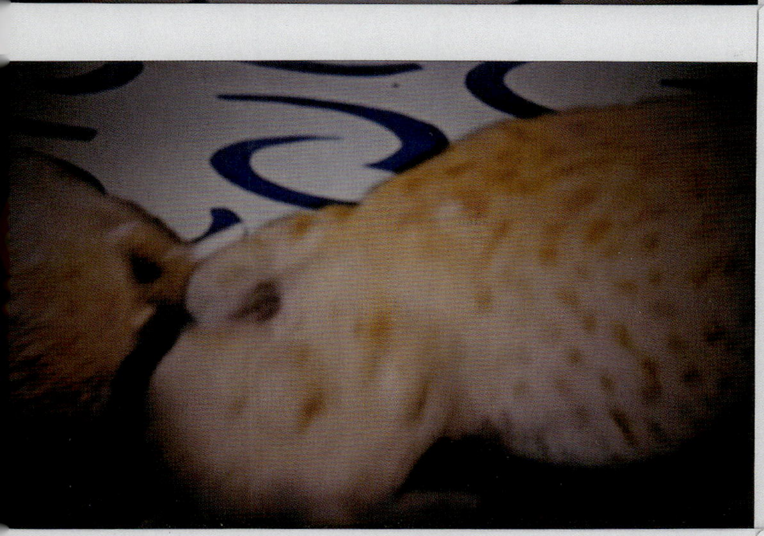
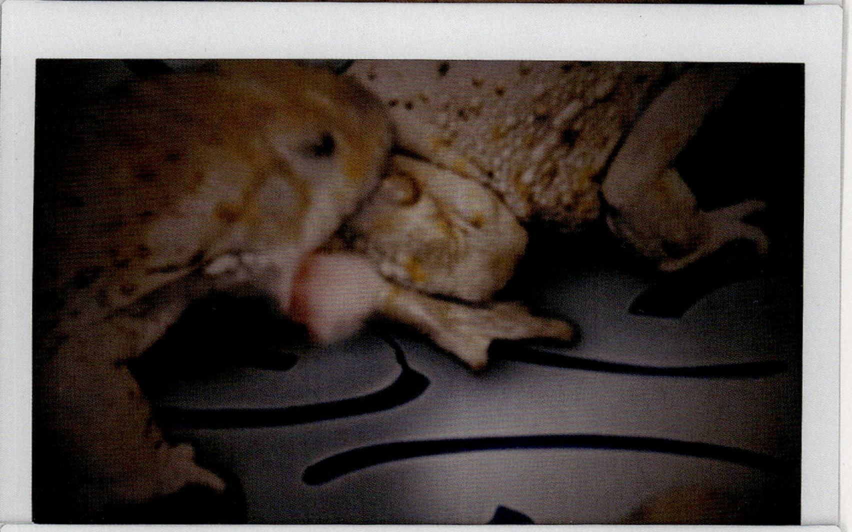
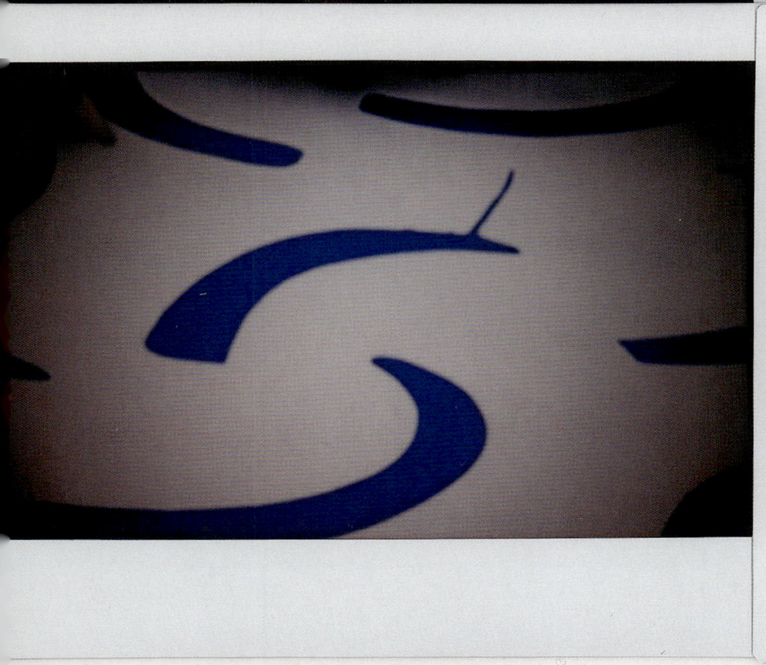
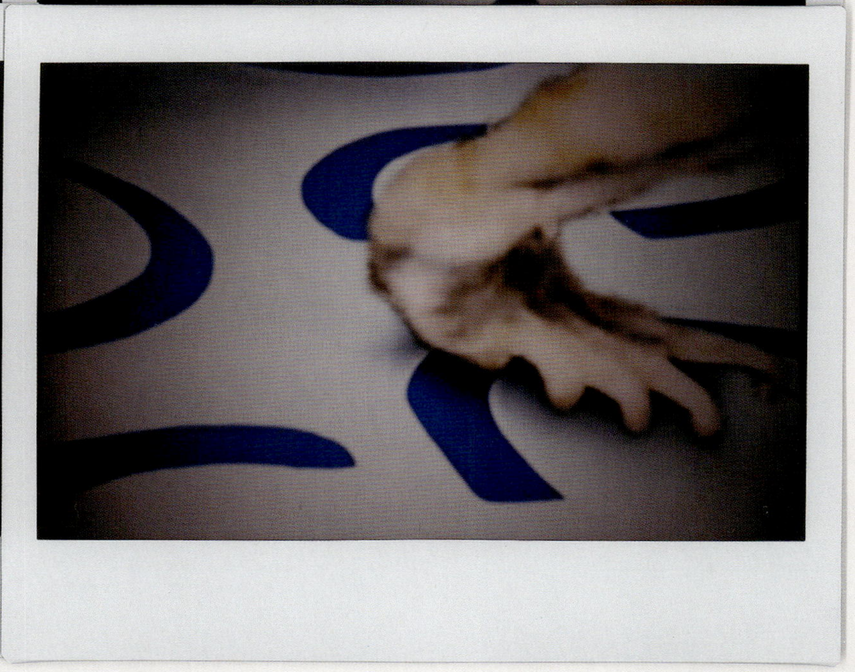

34

Radiation With Benefits

Lucy Beech (LB), Riar Rizaldi (RR)

A conversation between artists Lucy Beech and Riar Rizaldi who are both members of the Working With Waste research group.

LB With every high there's a low, and this is especially true when talking about radiation.

RR In relation to this I was thinking about the idea that nuclear energy is considered a *high temperature energy* because it produces so much energy with very small amounts of material. Anything related to nuclear energy is often related to low and high measurements, especially when working with pressure.

LB Have you heard of the acronym ALARA—As Low As Reasonably Achievable—which are guidelines for avoiding exposure to radiation that does not have a direct benefit to you. It makes me think about the distinction between 'radiation with benefits' and 'undesirable radiation'.

RR This is actually the first time I've heard of the term ALARA. Now I know it, from you.

LB It's interesting that the acronym changed over time. In the 1950s a version, ALARA meant As Low As *Practically* Achievable, and then As Low As *Readily* Achievable in the 1960s. Whether practically, readily, or reasonably achievable, low-level radioactivity is an inevitable byproduct of many industries—including those not necessarily associated with nuclear reactors. Another interesting acronym is NORM for Naturally Occurring Radioactive Materials that have to be cared for in line with their radioactive residues. You and I have a shared interest in the ways in which NORM waste arises from activities such as burning coal, gas and oil production, wastewater treatment, making and using fertilisers, or in the case of your field research, mining metal or extracting thorium for use in nuclear reactors. Did you encounter these acronyms whilst undertaking your research into mining in Bangka?

RR I actually encountered NORM protocol for the first time during my field research with a state-owned company that oversees a lot of the extractive business in a small island located in the west Indonesian archipelago called Bangka. I was researching the ecological impact of tin mining in the region.

LB So, you encountered radioactive residues as a byproduct of the mining industry? If so, how was the issue of low-level radiation being handled?

RR I did. And to deal with the growing concern about NORM wastes in this context the state-owned tin mining corporation PT Timah in Indonesia organised a safety management workshop in 2018, which was led by the International Atomic Energy Agency (IAEA). They discovered in this workshop that the tin mining area contains elevated natural minerals which are radioactive. News spread, because prior to this workshop people's concern about the mining activity was focused very much on ecological destruction. The workshop revealed radioactivity as another threat to the miners, especially those illegal artisanal miners. Geologists and nuclear physicists started to realise there were heavy deposits of thorium in Bangka, which is actually generated from the presence of tin ore. This discovery led to companies like ThorCon International (a company specialised in molten salt reactors) to lobby for a prototype nuclear reactor in Bangka.

LB So, a safety workshop initiated as a result of the miners' fears around radioactive exposure led to investments in thorium mining!

RR Yeah, it's almost like the NORM regulations and the workshop itself was like a pharmakon; opening the floodgate to other kinds of extractions. NORM protocol for many industries is about nuclear safety, but what happened in Indonesia was different.

LB This idea of the pharmakon is very interesting in the context of NORM wastes. I've also been exploring naturally occurring radiation produced from tin ore in the metal smelting industry. I was introduced to the subject via my mother who is a writer and retired environmental activist. When she was pregnant with me, she lived in a heavy mining and metal smelting area of the north of England, where metal waste from all over the world was recycled. My mother had become really preoccupied with the term 'sacrifice zone' and speculation over potential levels of radiation she and her community were exposed to via the smelting chimney at the heart of the community. This was in 1985 and prior to the formalisation of what we now understand to be NORM protocols for disposing radioactive residues from industrial processes. Her story is part of the paradigm shift which occurred in the UK (and of course globally) around attitudes to radioactive waste. The use of rivers and tidal flows as natural tools for evacuating radioactive waste to the sea was being strongly contested on the basis of environmental deterioration, declines in biological diversity, and even biological extinction that were observed in areas such as Hull where I grew up as a small child. Environmentalists were working with scientists (along with health workers, midwives, and community volunteers) to provide evidence for the need to instate 'safe zones' which could protect humans and aquaculture in the vicinity of metal smelting and nuclear power plants.

RR It's interesting that the standardisation of NORM is also always subject to change and updates.

LB As is the role that everyday people, workers, and environmental activists play in implementing those changes. For example, in my mum's story, which she actually wrote up into a screenplay, she was involved in consciousness raising via her midwife, who was collecting evidence on the way in which the toxicities were effecting children in the area… In Bangka were there also self-organised investigations of the radiation? What was the kickback from the wider community?

RR Yeah, there is a very strong anti-nuclear position in Indonesia and because of the discovery of radioactive thorium on the islands, the community in Bangka is still very worried that the island will be used for a nuclear power plant. But there are very interesting modes of resistance emerging on the island, including a small group of reactionary scientists working in tin mining who are focused on phytomining which is a form of nonhuman mining implemented by plants. The plant is genetically modified to syphon desired minerals from the ground soils. The plant is then cut and burned, and the burnt plant residue is extracted and used to produce pure material in the shape of ingot. So, these scientists are now genetically engineering new plants which could act in place of machinery extractions. This research exemplifies how future mining could be a slow process of using the lands as an apparatus to extract minerals. Their proposal is really interesting because it's also very speculative, yet actually quite feasible in terms of creating hyperaccumulators, or plants that do this work. Kale and broccoli, for example, have proved to be very good at sucking iron from the soil.

LB The use of plants to leech naturally occurring radioactive minerals makes me think about mineral evolution and the ways in which we might think of the Earth as an open system;

accumulating various irons and receiving celestial debris on a daily basis from space, which include meteorites, etc.

RR Totally, I'm very interested in the idea of mineral evolution which was proposed by astrobiologist Robert Hansan. Hansan works from the question: "Were all of Earth's minerals created before Earth's formation, during, or after?" The basic chemical elements of life—including rocks, minerals, thorium, radium and so on—are derived from atoms that were made in the deep interior of the sun and other stars where carbon and oxygen atoms are produced, along with nitrogen and phosphorus. These elements are synthesised via a nuclear reaction that takes place deep in the star's interior and are then thrown out into space by a supernova. Earth's formation is part of this process. In addition to this idea of the planet as an open system, I think there is a discussion to be had on the concept of native and non-native minerals on Earth which somehow determines the economy of space mining—although perhaps space mining is subject for another discussion!

LB So, is this also a way of thinking about panspermia?

RR The general idea of panspermia is that life is actually coming from outside the Earth. In this context, I think nuclear energy is an entity of panspermia. Minerals that can generate endless heat are doing so via cosmic processes rather than geological ones. Meteorite mineralogy for example is a fascinating subject in which it's stated that every 30 or 40 years, new minerals are found. There are maybe 6,000 chemical compounds that are actually now known—some discovered in the last 20 years. To come back to Hansan—he was talking about the evolution of science as also the evolution of minerals. We see in this example how science needs to be continually upgraded as the minerals evolve.

LB In the context of measuring toxicity and radiation exposure and thinking about evolution, you mentioned in one of our earlier conversations that human evolution may adjust to radioactivity and this will affect standardizations of high or low exposure, or even make such standardisation irrelevant. I am interested in hearing more about what you mean by that.

RR I was drawn to ideas of Russian cosmism, a philosophical movement in turn of the 20th century Russia which tapped into the idea of immortality by hacking the trajectory of human evolution and biomimicry to explore the potentiality of an organism that thrives in extreme environments. At the same time, I was interested in this ongoing research on the effect of radioactivity in animals and plants of contaminated zones like Chernobyl and Fukushima. Some of these animals have mutated, some are dead, and some survived with damaged DNA which eventually affects their genes, producing a generation with contaminated DNA. These animals you could say are adjusted to the radioactivity level of Fukushima or Chernobyl. I was wondering then, could this perhaps also apply to humanity? The more radiation we are exposed to, the more possibilities of human species adjusting to radioactivity. All of these speculations on the effects of high and low exposure to radioactivity are central topics in terms of space travel and DNA mutation which emerged since geneticists like Chris Mason put forward the idea of DNA evolution in relation to radioactivity and the human body. Perhaps high and low standardisations will become obsolete in the future and humans will live side by side with radioactive materials? This kind of idea resonates with the notion of longtermism.

LB Thinking about deep time processes and the sense of time more generally in the context of nuclear/atomic discourse, how does longtermism relate to the scope of atomic energy according to your research?

RR I think the cosmological scope of nuclear energy is interesting in terms of time and nonhuman connections to nuclear fission. The scientific discovery of nuclear fission is really important and fascinating. In fact, to this day, I cannot comprehend the idea that somehow humanity could split atomic energy. But I am also interested in the notion that nuclear fission occurs naturally over billions of years in the Earth's core. Perhaps you are familiar with the natural nuclear fission in Oklo, Gabon? Natural nuclear fission is a process that requires deep time. Long before the discovery of radioactivity and the possibility of splitting the atom, the long process of fission reaction in uranium deposits was activated through a deep time process of chemical reaction over the course of two billion years.

LB Did this natural nuclear fission provide evidence that long-term geologic storage of nuclear waste is feasible?

RR Yes, but also the deep time process of natural nuclear fission exemplifies the time it takes Earth to generate a radioactivity: a process which took approximately two billion years. As an artist and filmmaker the scope of time is always intriguing to me.

LB I agree, I'm fascinated by Marie Curie's discovery of radioactivity and how this opened up where scientists understood the Earth to be in history—I know you are too! I started researching polonium 210 (the radioactive isotope in which Curie observed radiation along with radium) because Polonium 210 were the radioactive isotopes found in the river system that my mother was documenting in the 1980s. I remember reading in Curie's diaries that her discovery of radiation forced her to recognise how limited her perception was of the world which surrounded her and that of future generations. Curie's diaries are still radioactive and have to be measured with a Geiger counter before and after use.

RR Curie's findings, especially in radium and polonium, opened up new ideas about time for many scientists during a period in which they were trying to grasp the complex inner structure and immense energy stored in atoms. Curie discovered large amounts of endless energy emitting from radium and recorded its capacity to generate endless heat.

LB So, how did this discovery revolutionise the way physicists were conceptualising time and energy?

RR Before the discovery of radioactivity many scientists believed that the Sun someday would dim. This was because they didn't know where the source of energy in the Sun was coming from. Scientists until that point had speculated mathematically based only on heat and temperature. When the discovery of radioactivity went public, scientists started to extend cosmical time scales.

LB So, geological practices for understanding time and the history of the Earth evolved into cosmic processes involving the Sun?

RR Yeah, and through the discovery of radioactivity, scientists were able to predict the cosmic scale of the future. Radioactivity also helped many scientists to measure carbon radioactivity through radiometric dating which eventually could generate a precise number of the absolute age of geological features, including the age of Earth, that eventually gave way to the idea of geological time scale.

LB It's also interesting that Curie named Polonium after Poland, her homeland, making Polonium the first element on the table with a politically charged name. Poland in 1898 remained partitioned among three empires: Russian, Austrian, and Prussian, and Curie used its naming as a means to shed light on the occupation.

RR For me, personally, the connection of radioactivity and time is also very political because after independence the political imagination of Indonesia was very entangled with nuclear discourse. The first president, Soekarno, was keen on the idea of implementing a nuclear power plan in the Indonesian archipelago. The archipelago is vast with thousands of islands so he thought nuclear power could cut the logistical nightmare of distributing energy whilst creating a long term vision for Indonesia as a state that could be run sustainably on nuclear energy. In the early '50s until mid-'60s his idea was really supported by both sides, American and Soviet. The International Atomic Energy Association also supported his proposal, and asked him to launch the country's own nuclear

Abandoned tin mining sites in Bangka Island. Image from Kasiterit, 2019.

agency Badan Tenaga Atom Nasional (founded in 1958). However, in the mid-'60s, the Southeast Asian region was a neo-colonial regime. Most of Indochina, especially Vietnam, was under American occupation and the British Empire also went back to Malaysia. He saw this as a threat, and he changed his idealistic longtermist nuclear power plant utopia into a site for manufacturing nuclear weapons. He built a close connection with China and this triggered America (and the West) in particular to stop him from developing nuclear weapons—which also ended in the coup. His career ended in the coup and the next regime was run by a military dictatorship that basically sold much of the land that contained radioactive minerals to the West, thus contributing to mineral extraction for the development of nuclear power.

LB What are the benefits of the archipelago as space for mining and producing nuclear energy?

RR It's safer to build a nuclear power plant in uninhabited islands detached from populated islands. But in the context of Soekarno, he was thinking a lot about logistics. Using coal as an energy resource would have cost more—as well as the need to transfer coal from one island to another. Building more coal-fired power plants was more logistically difficult than nuclear power plants for the whole archipelago distributing the electricity through a generator.

LB This example of Soekarno's attempted reinvention of the nuclear reactor as a site for manufacturing weapons represents one of the biggest fears of anti-nuclearism (along with of course the threat of climate change and the onset of natural disaster). Soekarno's inconsistency perfectly describes the need for the acknowledgement of uncertainty within contemporary nuclear narratives. It seems to me that much pronuclear rhetoric works from a quite aggressive veneer of certainty which seems to occlude these kinds of cases where political circumstances have the potential to change hands.

RR It makes me think of the history of the radiation symbol, the trefoil and the recent updates on this ionizing radiation warning symbol by International Atomic Energy Agency and International Standard Organisation. The symbol was first initiated in 1948 by Berkeley Radiation Laboratory, and in late 2000 apparently there was a survey that said many people in the world are not so familiar with the trefoil symbol. Thus, later in 2007, IAEA decided to revise the symbol using an additional skull to illustrate death. It fascinates me to think how the symbolism will evolve. I wonder whether the future human will be baffled with the variation of these symbols. Perhaps it feels similar to how we use cave paintings to understand a specific history.

LB The Dutch nuclear waste processing and storage company COVRA is also an interesting example, as they have become a beacon of hope for many pro-nuclear environmentalists due to the pride the organisation takes in their transparency. CORVA reflects the cultural appreciation of straight talking in the Netherlands. They explain on their website that it's valuable to communicate clearly what goes on inside the facility where waste is stored and cooled for 100 years before moving to a deep geological repository where it will remain radioactive for up to one million years. One way this has been put into practice is to make a climate controlled 'low level' nuclear waste storage bunker double up as storage space for the local art museums in the region. COVRA have created a loud statement that says nuclear waste is not something that must be forgotten or obscured, but transformed into heritage that needs to be taken care of (in the same way you would a tapestry or painting).

RR Have you ever found out what their intention in using art in this nuclear context?

LB Art seems to have been enlisted to aid in their process of clear communication…which, according to COVRA, makes the process more legible and thus ideally less contested. It seems to be a process of distillation where the presence of these artefacts function as a way of making the inexplicable timespan of the waste's radioactivity more contained or easily defined. But I wonder how COVRA's neatly sewn narrative of transparency, as open as it may appear, can account for any unforeseeable political or natural change to the environment (as we see so clearly in your earlier Soekarno example).

RR Yes, and as we know, no one predicted Fukushima.

LB I do think COVRA is opening up some of the misconceptions about radioactive waste as glowing green ghostbusters goo from nuclear reactors (which is also a focus of many pronuclear ecomodernists). Until I took the time to research NORM waste, I never really understood that industries like recycling, gas, oil, fertiliser production, even wastewater treatment all produce radioactive wastes that have to be cooled and stored (like radioactive waste) before being also moved to a geological repository for a further million years! This includes unexpected materials like medical waste and animal carcasses which are first reduced to ash through incineration and cast in concrete to contain their toxicity before sitting side by side with nuclear waste in spaces like COVRA.

RR They're not the deep geological repository. They're above ground, right?

LB Yes, and for the Netherlands, the longer term storage consignment will be a cooperation with another small country such as Belgium. We are living through a particularly interesting time regarding debates around nuclear longtermism. This month here in Germany, the last three nuclear power stations went off grid. On one side of Brandenburg gate, anti-atomic activists celebrated a win in a battle that has lasted 60 years, on the other side, pro-nuclear environmentalists were vehement that Germany should "PHASE OUT COAL AND GAS NOT NUCLEAR." The deep geological repository for low and intermediate nuclear waste called the Konrad repository that Germany has worked tirelessly to build will close indefinitely before its planned opening in 2027 due to such ideological rifts. This year, Finland opened the first repository for high level radioactive waste in the world and it will soon become mandatory for other countries to have their own. I was talking with someone in Germany who works with a group of engineers who are applying to close the Morsleben GDR mine-turned-nuclear repository (which once operated as a subterraneous arms production facility, and later a chicken farm). The process of closing the repository is an engineering puzzle (headed up by female engineers) that depends on ensuring the chosen materials will be water tight for 1 million years. It seems unthinkable, the task of speculating on the Earth's composition in a million year's time.

RR Shall we go to COVRA together?

LB Yes! Let's do it. The crazy thing is, I read somewhere that the art on view at COVRA are actually reproductions!

Last year in January, my boyfriend Pete and I took a trip to Mexico. After some days in Mexico City, we spontaneously decided to take a bus to Tepotzotlán, a small town about an hour away. Some years before, on our first trip together to Mexico, we had visited this town with a couple of friends, Annette and Axel. Pete had known Axel for a very long time, and he and Annette had been together for a couple of years. She had been staying in Tepotzotlán for a while as part of a writing residency called Under the Volcano, named after the Malcolm Lowry novel which was written during his stay in the region decades earlier.

That trip was magical, and we fell completely in love with this special place. So, on our return trip, we woke up in the morning, checked out of the hotel, and decided to go to the bus station. Soon we were on our way, and after an hour's ride and a melodramatic telenovela playing on the overhead screens, we arrived and set our stuff down at a little hotel in the town center.

As we set out, walking from our hotel towards the market square, I turned to Pete and exclaimed joyfully, "It's so wonderful here! The only thing missing is Axel and Annette!" We walked about a hundred meters more, and suddenly, standing right before us was Annette!

We were all completely in shock, laughing, smiling, and hugging, in utter disbelief of our luck to all be reunited here. After our excited greetings, we took a walk together down to a small grove of trees with a little bridge over a stream, and chatted about how we'd all been spending the last few years. Annette told us that she was now working in the field of psychedelic research and was organizing an interdisciplinary conference centered around this topic. I listened with rapt attention, full of curiosity about everything she was describing to us. At that time, I had just finished a long and difficult project, and was about to embark on an even bigger challenge. Taking psychedelics had been an important catalyst for changes in my life, and I had taken them every few years when I felt I was at a crossroads psychologically. Now I was at another such point. There was a certain feeling of destiny to this meeting, and I was excited to see where it might lead. We agreed to meet the next day for lunch.

Metabolism of 7-hydroxymitragynine in human plasma
Kratom
7-Hydroxymitragynine (Potent μ-opioid agonist)
Mitragynine pseudoindoxyl (Highly potent μ-opioid agonist)
Mitragynine (Moderate μ-opioid agonist)
Liver metabolism
Metabolism in blood
Time (min)
Mouse
Rat
Dog
Monkey
Human
Formation of unknown-1 (mitragynine pseudoindoxyl) upon 7-hydroxymitragynine incubation with the mouse, rat, dog, cynomolgus monkey, and human plasma. All values are plotted as mean ± SD (n = 3)
Kamble, Shyam, et al. ACS Pharmacology & Translational Science (2020). DOI: 10.1021/acsptsci.0c00075
UF College of Pharmacy UNIVERSITY of FLORIDA

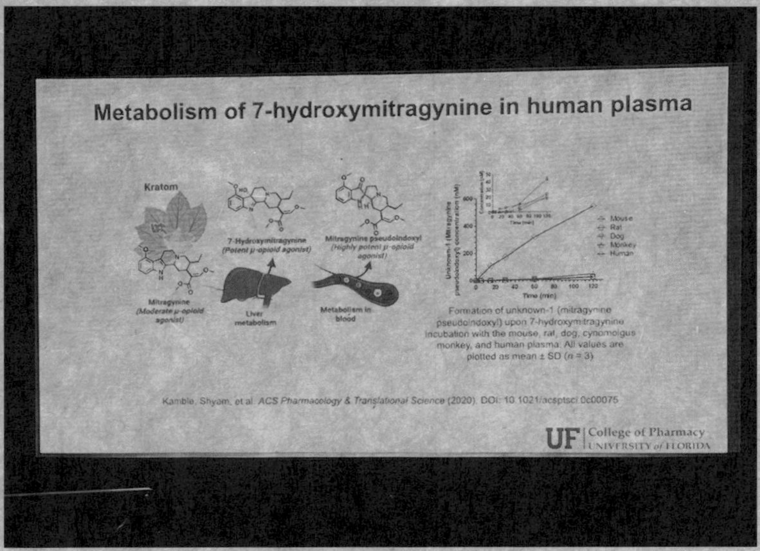

That day, we talked more about Annette's other occupations. It seemed that she was involved in an elite echelon of psychedelia. And while we listened to stories and descriptions of the kinds of events she was participating in, I asked if I might be able to attend the conference she was organizing that spring. She immediately accepted, and was truly excited about the prospect of us joining her there.

Months went by and my days were filled with exhibitions and projects, but Annette and I kept in contact about the conference. She sent me the program of the weeklong event, titled ESPD55, the acronym for Ethnobotanical Search for Psychoactive Drugs. A few names were familiar to me, and Pete also did a little bit of background research and watched a few interviews with some of the speakers. By the time May came around, Pete and I were very excited to make the journey there. We took the train to London, where we would meet the other participants and catch a bus all together to the conference, which was somewhere in the British countryside.

Bioorg Med Chem. 2010 July 1; 18(13): 4783-4792.
Synthesis and structure-affinity relationships of novel small molecule natural product derivatives capable of discriminating between serotonin 5-HT1A, 5-HT2A, 5-HT2C receptor types
Aplysinopsin are founds in a variety of marine organisms, A dinoflagellate from an anemone reportedly produced aplysinopsins.
but are also effective against tumors and roundworms (and MAO inhibition)
Sponges producing aplysinopsins:
-Thorecta aplysinopsis (named for this sponge)
-Verongia spengelii
-Dercitus
-Hyrtios erecta
-Smenospongia aurea
- other Thorectandra, Smenospongia and Verongula species
Aplysinopsin pharmacophore and numbering:
R1 and R2 alkylation is important,
As is R4 and R5 halogen substitution
6-F derivative
5-HT2A>5-HT2C
6-chloro
5-HT2C selectivity 602X>5-HT2A
6-Br derivative
5-HT2C selectivity 45X>5-HT2A
5,6-dichloro derivative (UNT-TWU-22)
5-HT2C selectivity 2170X>-5-HT2A
6-bromo-2'-de-N-methylaplysinopsin
5-HT2C selectivity 40X > 5-HT2A)

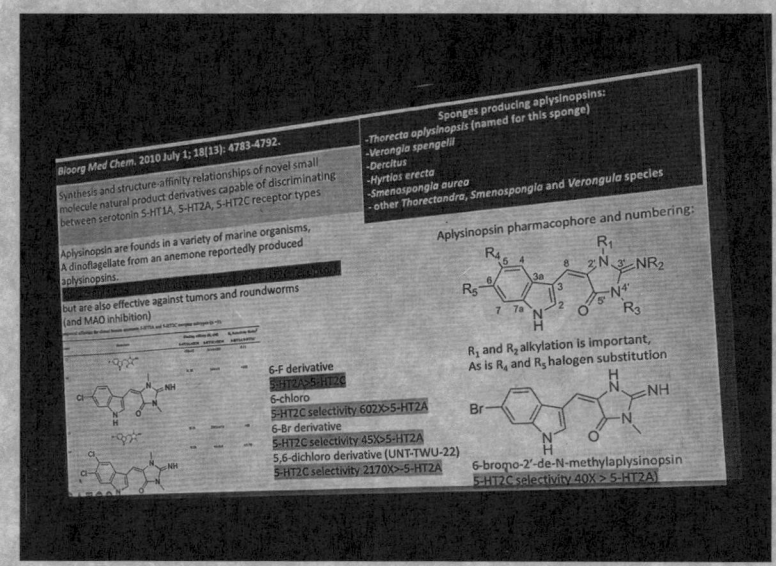

The meeting place was an art gallery in the middle of London, and when we arrived, everyone's suitcases were in the first room, and there was a lunch spread. The first people we met were an older couple—an ethnobotany professor, Mark Merlin, and his wife who had flown in all the way from Hawaii. Their exhaustion didn't impact their friendliness though, and we soon discovered that we had studied at the same university in California, and he had even grown up in the same neighborhood where I had lived!

INTEGRAL PROJECTION MODELS: A ROAD MAP FOR SUSTAINABLE AYAHUASCA PRODUCTION

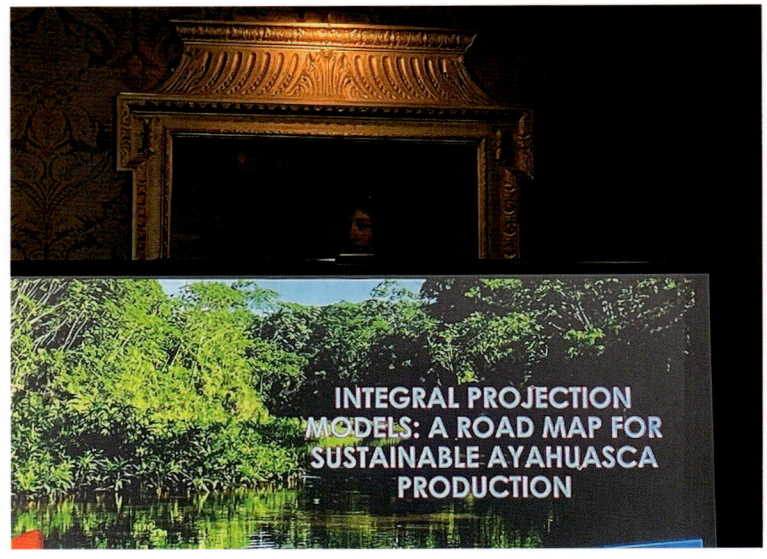

We also met a former student of his, Michael Coe, also living in Hawaii, who would be presenting for the first time at the conference and was very excited and nervous to share his research. He would frequently express gratitude for being there, and was generally brimming with positivity. I think we were both a bit overwhelmed by his sunny disposition; it was a bit of a shock for us, having come from Berlin.

We went outside for a while and chatted with a slightly more skeptical person, Brian Pace, whose down-to-earth attitude made us feel a little more comfortable. He introduced himself as a reporter for a journal called Psymposia, which he described as an industry watchdog. Pete and I were so naïve and new to this scene that we said we were surprised that there was already an established industry surrounding psychedelics, not just an underground market. He paraphrased some recent articles they had published about psychedelics being co-opted by the right wing in America, which seemed completely contradictory to me at that time.

Soon it was time to board our bus, and after about a two or three hour drive, we arrived at a historic stately home, surrounded by vast manicured gardens. Here the bus was met by the hosts, a young couple who had inherited and restored this enormous property. We wandered the grounds a bit, looked at an ancient Lebanese cedar tree planted within a huge lush lawn, and then joined a small reception with all the participants. One of the guests had brought a special gift for the hosts: some vines from his garden of Banisteriopsis Caapi and leaves of Psychotria Viridis, the two main components of Ayahuasca. With jubilant glee, our host, Michael, and Pete and I rushed to the greenhouse to put the plants into soil. As we hurriedly worked in the vegetable greenhouse under fading light, I imagined this could be an episode of the perennial BBC classic *Gardener's World*.

Cone of Uncertaint
Mushrooms N. Africa (Tassili Plateau)
Early Shamanic use of Psychedelics for:
- Healing
- Social Cohesion
- Reverence
- Knowledge Transfer
- Purpose
Pop. Density <25/sqmi
Mushrooms W. Europe (Selva Pascuala)
Ergot W. Europe (Early Christian use)
Jesuit Order Mushrooms, Yopo, Peyote brought back to Europe
Reefer Madness Released
Pop: 128M, 34/sqmi
UN Convention / US Controlled Substances Act
Pop: 197M, 52/sqmi
Pop: ~62M, 36/sqmi (excluding Ottoman Empire, Russia)
Concern of Exogenous Threats to Social Order, Cultural & Political Influence
Pop. Density 30-35/sqmi
Cannabis, Aconite Xia & Shang, China
Pop: ~13M, 27/sqmi
Pop: ~38M, 31/sqmi
Regulation or Suppression by Dominant Power
Pop. Density >50/sqmi
Endogenous Threats to Social Order
Need for Healing
Lack of Social Cohesion
Nostalgia for Days Past
Data-overload, Knowledge shortfall
Crisis of Purpose
Pop. Density >85/sqm
Peyote, Mushrooms, Ayahuasca N. America and S. America
Pop: ~61M, 51/sqmi
China
Eurasia
Western Europe
Americas
Kykeon Ancient Greece (Temple of Eleusis)
Pop: ~1M, 14/sqmi
Temple of Eleusis Destroyed
Pop: ~65M, 38/sqmi
5000 BCE
4000 BCE
3000 BCE
2000 BCE
1000 BCE
500 BCE
250 BCE
0
100
300
1000
1500
1900
1940
1970
2020

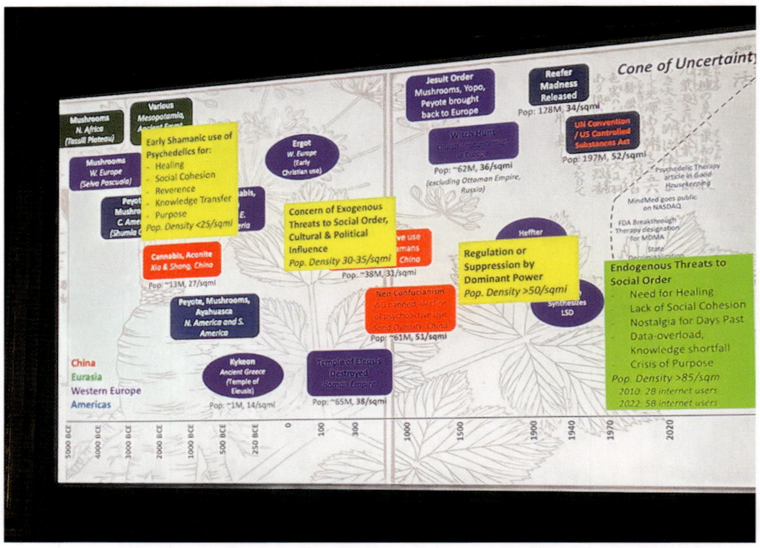

The next morning the conference began with an opening speech by Dennis McKenna, whose academy was hosting the entire event. McKenna himself is an ethnobotanist, and brother of the '60s counterculture figure Terence McKenna, and was a personal friend and mentor to most of the people attending. He introduced the keynote speaker, Monica Gagliano. She described a behavioral conditioning experiment she made on pea plants. However, the results of the experiment were inconclusive, which led her to state that the plants have a deeper consciousness of their own that humans can't truly understand. Her lecture sparked a vigorous debate among the audience regarding the scientific method in general, where things got rather heated between the more spiritually-directed intellectuals and the more standard institutional specialists such as the mycologists in the room. While the hard scientists criticized her lack of verifiable results, she insisted on the importance of listening to the plants directly. Several times over the next few days, when people discussed the concept of plant teachers, or that plants were speaking to them, I understood it in a metaphorical sense, but they corrected me and others that they were speaking literally.

The next speaker, Chris McCurdy, a pharmacologist from the University of Florida, came onstage and thanked Dr. Gagliano, and said that his research was similar in some ways to hers. He continued that when he started working on Mitragyna Speciosa, that the plant found him. He had been studying naturally occurring analgesics with the National Institute on Drug Abuse and was first concentrating on Salvia Divinorum until this plant came to the forefront of his thinking. He described how it is used traditionally in southeast Asia as a tea called Kratom, and that the combination of active compounds—rather than each one in isolation—is responsible for its effectiveness as both a stimulant and painkiller. In pharmacology, the standard procedure to study any plant medicine is to isolate its alkaloids and purify them, and test which brain receptors are activated by these compounds.

Dr. McCurdy described how, one day in the shower, he realized that it made no sense to do this when the tea was a "whole symphony orchestra, so why take each instrument out?" He then described the deep research he and his team were doing together with botanists at the university, to understand the mysteries of this fascinating plant. The lecture became more and more technical, with all sorts of molecular formulas, but what stuck with me was that it is used widely already by heroin and methamphetamine addicts to lessen their withdrawal symptoms when trying to reduce their use of those drugs, even though Kratom's mechanism of action works differently in the brain and is nowhere near as dangerous or addictive in itself. Most importantly, it does not cause respiratory depression, which is the main cause of death among opiate users. He proceeded to describe the various experiments they are doing to investigate its potential to make a medication for treating opioid use disorder. I was absolutely riveted by this talk, and the depth of Dr. McCurdy's research.

Over the next few days, many of the talks came back to ideas about fundamental methodology. Whereas modern pharmacology is premised on isolating particular molecules, specifically alkaloids, traditional medicine uses whole plants and combinations of plants to produce its effects. On the third day of the conference, Elaine Elisabetsky, an ethnopharmacologist working in Brazil, gave a presentation that addressed these issues directly. She talked about all of the pitfalls in her discipline and the difficulties of field research. All of the knowledge in ethnopharmacology or ethnobotany comes from listening to indigenous doctors, but her colleagues were not being attentive enough. They often didn't understand the relationship of trust between these village doctors and their patients, or listen to their diagnoses with enough care. She gave the example of a doctor she had interviewed in the Amazon, who described an illness caused by possession of a female water spirit, who dragged the patient down, made them toss and turn and foam at the mouth. In the worldview of this culture, these symptoms were associations with rivers and would be embodied by a spiritual antecedent. In the western view, these would be descriptive of a grand-mal seizure, which means that the vegetal preparation used to treat this condition would be a likely treatment for epilepsy.

Dirty Pictures
Gateway to Psychoactive Structure Activity Relationships
Pattern: Aromatic ring with two carbons stretch to nitrogen of an amine
Melatonin
N,N-Dimethyltryptamine (DMT)
MDA
6-APDB
Adrenaline
Adrenochrome
Mescaline
Bromo-dragonFLY

Elisabetsky described how most medicine is developed "bench to bed," meaning that only after extensive testing would it be administered to a patient. Traditional medicine goes "bed to bench"—its efficacy is already known, and it's analyzed in the laboratory to unpack its mysteries. And many of these medicinal plants abound in mysteries.

After Dr. McCurdy, Michael Coe was the next speaker, and he gave a presentation of his field survey of Banisteriopsis Caapi within a few sites in the Amazon rainforest. The locations of these plants are carefully guarded, because the plant is in danger of extinction due to overharvesting. The worldwide popularity of Ayahuasca has significantly diminished the varieties of these plants in the wild. And while strains of these plants may look identical to a western scientist, to indigenous people they are considered as completely different varieties, each with their own properties known from experience.

So many of the lectures were fundamentally about this exact dilemma—trying to bridge different orders of experience to understand the changes in perception these plants are able to bring about. In all likelihood, Pete and I were the only people in the room who hadn't actually drank Ayahuasca before. And to everyone else, they were trying to describe, in the frameworks and language from their various disciplines, the ineffable and the sublime. Some gave deeply personal accounts of their experiences taking psychedelics, of cleaving their ego away from their perception of the world, and how this came to aid all their other life pursuits. One self-described "visionary scientist," Bruce Damer, gave an account of how a lifetime of psychic journeying had culminated in his development of an astrobiological theory of how life had developed from cellular fragments in the warm and murky fluids of the young Earth.

That same day, Paul Stamets, the famous old-head mycologist in the room, had given a passionate lecture about his lifetime of research on psilocybin. He concluded his talk with an emotional plea—that he believes psilocybin makes nicer and better people. This came after he showed sociological studies proving that psychedelic users had decreased violent behavior and that hallucinogens were effective in treating opioid use disorder, which he tearfully said had caused a crisis in his own family. These studies were elaborated on by Michelle St. Pierre, a PhD student in sociology writing her dissertation on psychedelic use

$n(y,t+1) = \int_{\Omega} K(y,x)n(x,t)dx$ (IPM)
Growth
Fertility
Flowering
Probability
Time
Germination
Survival

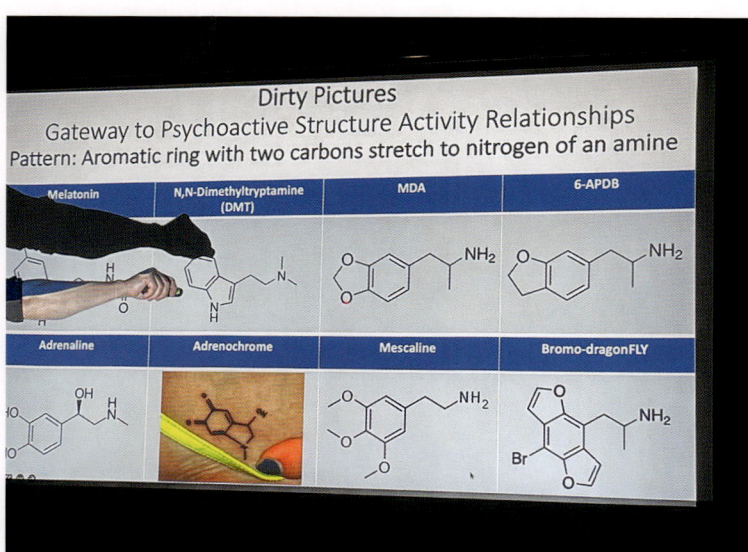

among prisoners, and David Nutt, an esteemed psychologist working on clinical trials with entheogens and psychedelics for alcohol and drug use disorders.

In general, everyone speaking at the conference held these substances in the highest respect and felt they had tremendous healing potential. Rather than being an agent of escapism, they allowed people to confront and work through their problems. What concerned most people was the legislation of these substances, or the co-opting of them by the wrong actors, that would corrupt their power. But it's already too late, and many of the speakers talked about the destruction of the rainforest, overharvesting of traditional medicinal plants, and the loss of indigenous ways of knowledge, as well as the use of psychoactive plants in societally harmful ways. Some worried about the pitfalls of legalization, or medicalization, and one speaker made an elaborate chart of a sort of idealized psychedelic landscape, the best and worst outcomes that could happen from the course things are taking now.

The most interesting moments of the conference happened when there were unplanned correspondences between various lectures. On the first day, Jonathan Lu gave a talk speculating about the use of psychoactive plants and fungi in China. He gave a sweeping cultural history of the country, laden with grand theories about cultural psychology, not just in China but also in comparison to simultaneous movements around the world. He also introduced some historical figures important to traditional Chinese medicine. Finally, he gave an account of some mystery boletes which are frequently consumed in Sichuan province in the form of a soup.

The next evening, Colin Domnauer and Bryn Dentinger, two mycologists from the University of Utah, reported on these very same mystery boletes. They followed up on reports from China of poisonings from psychoactive mushrooms, where the patients had reported seeing many *tiny people*. This elicited many jokes from the audience, but nonetheless as the lecture continued it was clear that Jonathan Lu and the mycologists needed to compare notes. During the question and answer section, the famed mycologist Giuliana Furci, who had traveled to the conference with her colleague Merlin Sheldrake, pressed the scientists onstage, and gradually introduced a new conundrum about the taxonomy of fungi in general. Because, while other types of organisms evolve over generations, or vertically within a *family tree*, fungi are so difficult to classify because these changes can occur horizontally in a taxonomic chart—meaning, within the very same generation. Therefore, classifying fungi becomes an elusive exercise, when one single organism can change species within its own lifetime.

This problem of classification in some ways overtook the whole conference, and was the same thing that made it generative. With so many experts from different fields all looking centrally at one topic, that topic invariably changed itself, as well as changing the perceptions of all of the participants (hopefully for a long time). For me, being engaged in these conversations felt adjacent to a kind of high—thoughts of limitless potentiality, of being transported to vastly different places and states of mind, all of these things happened to me during those few days.

It would be nice to imagine that people could also evolve into different species within one lifetime, and that this conference would bring about deeper changes in consciousness in everyone there. At the same time, people's egos were still very much present and directing their behavior, no matter how much they had tried to kill those egos with Ayahuasca. I'm still left with many questions, doubts, and skepticism, as much as I do believe that these substances can help lead to many personal insights. So, even though I haven't actually become a *psychonaut* since then, it was wonderful to bask in their glow and have a contact high for those few days.

Tang Han

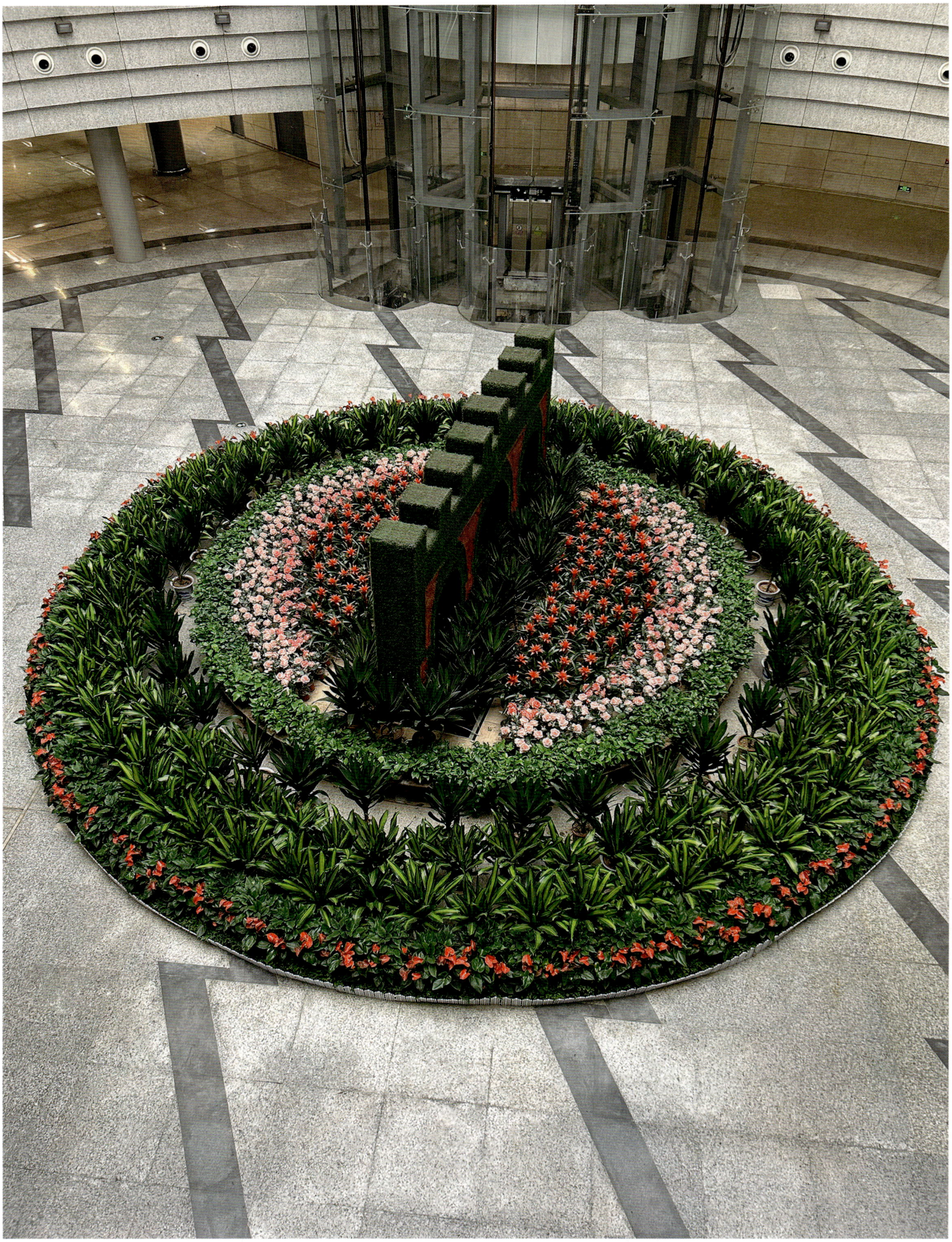

Towers of Hope

Christiane Blattmann

Did you know bullets used to be fabricated in *shot towers*, on top of which workers dropped molten lead through mesh? Thanks to surface tension and gravity, perfect missile spheres landed in a water basin on the tower's ground after their freefall.

Halfway through our art studies, my partner Jannis and I applied for a substantial grant from the city of Hamburg, awarded for the completion of projects in public space. We were a more affordable option for funding that, at the time, might have typically paid for a rusty Richard Serra sculpture or, as far as German cities were concerned, some huge granite blocks split by sculptor Ulrich Rückriem. We proposed building a concrete sculpture that would serve as an exhibition venue. Composed of cubic elements—two walls, three floor slabs, a stele that looked vaguely like an altar and two towers—our proposed open space stretched over a width and height of about four metres. Once the jury gathered to select projects, a woman from the city's arts council called my mobile phone with a question. They were wondering if our proposal was a joke. "No," I told her, "it actually isn't." And we got the funding.

In retrospect, the most surprising factor was that we were given funding to complete a big project without stating any conceptual goals other than venturing into the unknown. We wanted to work out what the project was about while undertaking it, not anticipate an impact in language. After all, who could have predicted the implications of a sculpture claiming to be exhibition space? We simply wanted to find out what an idea entailed in reality. We held 18 shows in the space, which we titled Betongalerie/Türme der Hoffnung (Concrete Gallery/Towers of Hope). The first part of its name was our working title, a blunt description. As this was still not satisfactory, and for fear of the blank page, we just wrote down anything that came to our mind resembling the name of a venue.

In the Towers of Hope, together with fellow artists and prospective gallerists and curators, friends, and neighbours, we showed large-format paintings on tiles, which we auctioned off per piece for a good cause; we showed the structure Christo/ Jeanne-Claude-style, wrapped in rubbish bags; we produced a four-act play; screened short films; turned the space back into a sculpture; planted a garden in the frozen ground where the fathers of artists gave a speech about gardening and raising sons; put on a piece made up entirely of the opinions of some 200 neighbours; turned the towers into a temple while providing a firework show at midnight on New Year's Eve; transformed the space into a car over whose speakers we presented an audio programme, while the temperature dropped below -5; massaged bodybuilder bronze cream into the concrete corpus after the site was turned into a platform for public speeches and book exchange.

According to Maggie Nelson, "art is characterized by the indeterminacy and plurality of the encounters it generates,"[1] and we felt strongly that this indeterminacy would have been lost had we pre-formulated what we wanted the project to accomplish. And we never could have anticipated the achievements that eventually ensued. For both of us, and possibly for some of the artists and other contributors with whom we have collaborated, the project has had a profound impact on our understanding of what art can do. At the risk of sounding too grand, it's made us think about how something that does not reveal its intentions (perhaps because they are not clear-cut), how something that cannot be fully defined (possibly because no definition pre-exists), opens a window of freedom, a surprising capacity for agency in both viewers and makers. Concerning the viewers, the project was a constant site of re-negotiation because people open-heartedly offered their opinions, since the site we had chosen for our work was also theirs. Both sides—makers and public—had a funny curiosity about each other's choices and reactions. Each time, for instance, we were installing or de-installing, passers-by informed us whether what we did was art or not. Likewise, the local tabloid press titling the project a "public toilet" was part of that aspect of art's status which Jacques Rancière describes as a third thing between people, whose meaning "is owned by no one, but which subsists between [artist and spectator], excluding any uniform transmission, any identity of cause and effect."[2]

Projecting into the future, asking what a work of art intends on *doing*, can be challenging to avoid. Ever since building Betongalerie, I've written many applications while trying to heed the warnings of my tweaking guts telling me not to fix something on paper which would later determine my thoughts or agency in the project. If only art were excluded from a Western obsession with the future. I wonder if we could re-learn a way of reception that focuses on what we perceive right before us rather than thinking about the effect an object or project is purported to achieve. In this regard, it might be helpful to think of expectations or hope as a signifier in the transition from the pre-modern and tradition-bound to the future-oriented society. Or, as Terry Eagleton phrases it, "from timeless metaphysical truths to the historically open-ended." He continues, "Modernity is a question of viewing the present in the light of its future, and thus in the light of its potential negation. Essence is now expectation. What defines a phenomenon, in a reversal of linear evolution, is the inner form that inflicts it toward the as yet unrealized. In a Benjaminesque inversion, it is its future that determines its present."[3]

In a Year of the Tower

Last spring, I went to a tarot reading. Francesca, my card master, told me I was entering a year of the Tower. The card in question shows a tower built on rough cliffs with flashes of lightning striking and flames bursting from its orifices. Left and right of the tower's erection, two figures are falling from a great height. Unlike other tarot cards with a dark twist to an otherwise optimistic reading—such as the Devil or the Hanged Man—the Tower has a less favourable reading to offer, except to suggest that after a period of devastating destruction, one will be left with nothing but the bare essentials and will come to know the relevant constituents of a life: materially and ideally. I pushed the reading to the furthest corner of my consciousness, asserting to myself that it was only soothsaying. Six months later, when life had been a bumpy ride, Anja asked me for a contribution to this issue: 'high'. Given my ceaseless interest in architectural topics and, lately, twisted fascination with high-rise buildings, I thought about writing a text on skyscrapers. As I began my research on tall buildings, all of a sudden, I *did* remember the card.

From about my birthday onwards, events seemed to be choreographed in a mysterious chain reaction. The first pearl lined up at an appointment in Brussels' town hall where, after seven years of living between Belgium and Germany, I wanted to commit and have a real, official life. I was excited to finally register and brought an armful of elaborate paperwork, imagining how I would surprise them with my excessive preparation. But the date was quick: they told me I needed to earn more money in Belgium, and there was nothing they could do except give me another three months to prove a decent local income. I felt like that tower myself—shaking with eruptions, my windows clattering. The truth was, I was not expecting any money in the coming months, and it was only now that I realised that I had been fuelled by hope for a long time.

Hope

Hope is the state of permanent suspension in which one waits for the occurrence of a certain, expected positive event, which, however, does not yet happen. While hoping, money is invested, resources are mobilised materially and mentally, promises are made, and networks established. In short: investments are made in an anticipated upcoming event. The contemporary crux, as found, for instance, in realms of freelance occupation: because there are so many hopes, and one permanently assures oneself that a single non-occurring event is part of the game, one hardly notices the disappointment because one is already busy with the next application. Is hope the fuel we need in order to exist in such inhospitable working conditions? Or does hope—as delay of real events—prevent us from making decisions that might allow us to feel good here and now?

As is well known, hope marks a central Christian virtue. Nonetheless, I wonder if this particular virtue of expecting/speculating about positive events in the future and incurring debts in the present moment has helped lay the groundwork for the current Western economic system. As much as religious hope might provide a railing to hold on to, it does create dependency. Unlike desire, a robust hope does not simply glance at a future contentment above the abyss of the present, one might argue in its favour, but has a foretaste of its fulfilment with a certain euphoria setting in. The firm belief in fulfilled narratives of achievement and—along with hope—other virtues, such as diligence and discipline, have a secure place in Christian tradition. Eschatology, which implies the primacy of the future over the present, is one of the central categories of Jewish Christianity. "God is not yet, but is yet to be."[4] Major religions agree on this outlook as the virtue of hope, yet Buddhism views it with suspicion, and a famous Lojong slogan rejects it completely: "Abandon any hope of fruition. Don't get caught up in how you will be in the future, stay in the present moment."[5]

Terry Eagleton notes that "hope, like desire as such, is the way in which the human animal is nonidentical with itself, its existence an eternal not-yet, its substance a kind of suspension."[6] This eternal "not-yet" reminds me of Kafka's "not-yet" motive in *Before the Law*, also known as *The Parable of the Doorkeeper*. In it, a man from the country seeks entry to the law through a gate guarded by a doorkeeper. Despite the man's insistence, the guard informs him that he cannot enter—yet. Access is not strictly denied but permanently suspended, even though the door is wide open. The man eventually dies after years and years of waiting in front of the door. Is the story of hope also a story about access? Not access in a spatial sense, but in a temporal one. On the other hand: do we have tools to take on challenges without hope? Expecting an outcome objectively: it could be a yes, it could as well be a no. Desire is always at risk of being disappointed.

Friedrich Nietzsche wrote about hope in reference to Pandora's box: "Zeus did not wish man, however much he might be tormented by the other evils, to fling away his life, but to go on letting himself be tormented again and again. Therefore he gives Man hope—in reality, it is the worst of all evils because it prolongs the torments of Man."[7]

On one of the more troublesome days, I called my friend Stacy to confess that I had to cancel a trip to New York, where I was going to stay with her. Even though I had already bought the plane tickets, it seemed like it might not be a good idea to travel while I was broke to a city where the prices for everything had skyrocketed. How would I enjoy the trip, especially since I could handle the essential tasks of the journey remotely? Stacy is a great friend and her reaction was very warm and understanding. She had some advice for me and asked if I had heard of visualization. "You have to imagine yourself in the situation that you desire to be in. Your goal. Think of how you would be, what you would do, where you would be and what you would look like if you reached that goal—in the greatest detail possible." This did not match with my new conviction about abandoning hope. But Stacy insisted it was not quite the same: it's not about hope—it's about making yourself understand what will be if you are there! You essentially skip hope! I got confused. By the end of the call, I felt consolidated by the warmth of friendship and someone genuinely listening. I really couldn't see myself embracing the visualization concept, yet if it had helped Stacy, then it couldn't be wrong altogether...

Visualization

- Be a Thermostat or a Thermometer: The thermostat responds to the environment. The thermometer sets the temperature and creates the desired condition. For example, if you're trying to lose weight, you might create a vision board of images of your goal body. Put it somewhere so that you can see it regularly. This works similarly to a goal visualization and analytics dashboard commonly used in business. That which is measured and monitored is improved!
- Winning and Achieving: Another effective visualization technique in a physical environment is to write yourself a check (if your goals are monetary in nature). For example, if you want to become a millionaire by age 40, you can write a check to yourself for one million dollars and have it framed. Most of the time, the best way to utilise visualization is to picture a single outcome; you win the race, you lose the weight, you get the promotion, etc. But it may also be helpful to visualize multiple potential outcomes.
- Avoid Negativity: What are all the ways this could pan out? What are the best-case and worst-case scenarios? Again, this is a way to moderate your fears. Just don't spend too long visualising negative outcomes, or they may come to dominate the narrative. Always shift back to a more positive mindset.
- Create Goal Pictures: Another powerful visualization technique is to create a photograph or picture of yourself with your goal, as if it were already completed. If one of your goals is to own a new car, take your camera down to your local auto dealer and have a picture taken of yourself sitting behind the wheel of your dream car. If your goal is to visit Paris, find a picture or poster of the Eiffel Tower and cut out a picture of yourself and place it into the picture.

The Swiss writer Robert Walser (1878–1956) lies dead in the snow.
He died on December 25, 1956, while walking in the vicinity of Herisau, Canton Appenzell.

Not long after speaking with Stacy, I was on the phone with my friend Anja, who wanted to know how my text for Pfeil was going. When we first chatted a little, I told her what I had learnt about visualisation and how I doubted the concept. It turned out that Anja was already practicing the technique, as instructed by her yoga teacher. Nevertheless, she offered a different take on it and told me about the death of Robert Walser. After a lavish lunch on Christmas day 1956, the writer left the Swiss sanatorium where he had been living as a patient for many years to go hike in the snow. Walser loved long, solitary walks. The exact circumstances of his death are unclear, but it is believed that he may have suffered a heart attack or hypothermia while out in the cold. A passerby discovered his body the next day. The dramatic incident instantly evoked an eerie reminiscence to a scene in his first novel, *Geschwister Tanner*. In the story, the description of the poet Sebastian's death in the snow accurately anticipates that of the author 50 years later.

Vertigo

Through my tower-tinted glasses, fulfilled prophecies bring before my inner eye J.G. Ballard's grotesque, surreal (yet all the more realistic) novel *High-Rise*. Its protagonist is a towering apartment building, freshly designed for middle-class and upper-middle-class tenants as a self-contained community with all the amenities they could need. However, the architecture itself has a strange influence on its inhabitants, imprinting its hierarchical design on their behaviour, first causing the residents to lose touch with the outside world and then clogging them into cliques which stage wars against the respective lower classes as the high-rise descends into chaos and violence.

The expectation of social upwards mobility is engrained in the archetype of the tower. In the material world, towers are home to extremes of the social spectrum: social tenements are tower-shaped, as are banks, offices, and hyper-contemporary forms of luxury dwelling. However, the nature of power symbolised in the erections in a cityscape has changed since the watchtowers of pre-modern times. Part of fortifications or demarcation walls: defence mechanisms and vantage points which regulated access or were rock-faced reminders of a prevailing hierarchy. These towers were also shaped by their practical functions; prison towers, water towers, siege towers, lighthouses, bell towers, minarets and clock towers. By contrast, in today's satellite-monitored and software-controlled environment, the tower is less functional and more symbolic than ever. In his book *Vertical*, Stephen Graham explores the relationship between social class and verticality in the built environment, highlighting the ways in which the tower has been used to reinforce social hierarchies and power structures. He suggests that the symbolism of the tower may be a reflection of our own psychological preoccupations with power and social status rather than a reflection of the functional needs of the built environment.

With modernism in the 20th century, the tower became a typology for social and affordable housing. The rise of steel-framed construction, elevators, and industrialised prefabrication fused with modernist urban ideas resulted in elevated apartment blocks being widely celebrated as powerful forces of social and economic modernization in response to industrial poverty, rapid urbanisation, and the mass strategic bombing of cities. Lifting the urban masses up into the light, sun, and air of functionalist towers would bring social and moral improvement to 'lower' life.

Yet, then came backlash and critique: high-rise towers were seen more and more as the embodiment of the lowest end of the social ladder, and no one wanted the symbol thereof to shape the silhouette of cities. High-rise housing was increasingly rejected in favour of giving working-class residents a ground-level space that could be surveyed and controlled.

As further consequence, mass social housing projects were largely undermined by processes of neo-liberalization, and vertical housing transformed into investment opportunities, primarily office towers and luxury apartments. This created a new type of city where previously only the small area above the surface could be commodified and leased. But now, air itself can be monetized and enclosed into rising towers. So much money is floating in the market in need of investment opportunities that it has caused housing to transform from its most basic function of providing accommodation into a lucrative investment strategy. The rise of super skinny towers as the ultimate assets has brought the symbolism of the tower to a maximum level of abstraction. In this new urban landscape, the value that towers signify has become distorted and disassociated from their original functions.[8]

Post Hope

The lighthouse and 'the tower' play a central role in Jeff VanderMeer's *Southern Reach* trilogy. In the story, the latter is a vertical underground tunnel accessed through a spiral staircase that leads deep beneath the Earth, and yet the novel's main character, the Biologist, insists it is a tower. In *Annihilation*, the series' first volume, we learn that both towers are located at the heart of Area X, a restricted zone where mysterious flora and fauna, as pristine as disturbing, have taken over: unleashed nature is spreading inexorably. Expeditions have been undertaken to find answers, draw maps, and understand the strange landscape, yet their participants either never return or change in uncanny ways. The lighthouse is a tangible, built, phallic manifestation, while the underground tower is a phantasmagoric sensation which seems to lead into the protagonists' innermost mental and psychological depths and paranormal states. In a world where natural forces prevail, they remain the only distinct human imprints.

VanderMeer's novels count among the literary genre of the New Weird, in which ecologically dystopian scenarios are often conceived in the form of speculative fiction. However, it has been debated whether the word 'weird' is appropriate or ethical given the severity and scale of the ecological problems of the Anthropocene or whether it conveys implications too cute for its true gravitas. Writer Kaisa Kortekallio argues that we find a sense of vertigo in New Weird novels, building on research in ecology to claim that the continuous transmutations of ecosystems are philosophically just as radically unknowable as Area X. She suggests that "groundlessness could thus be mapped as a particularly ecological feeling." Furthermore, she claims that "the sense of vertigo at the edge of weird ecologies marks an ongoing disintegration and reconfiguration of subjectivity. As the masterful, purely human subject quickly loses its viability as a lived condition, fiction begins to sketch and suggest new templates for experience."[9]

In *The White Lotus*, a 2021 Netflix comedy-drama, Paulina enters the scene in the first episode sporting a T-shirt emblazoned with POST HOPE in bold letters across her chest. The teenage protagonist and her friend Olivia are representative of Generation Z; headstrong, reading Nietzsche,

Freud, and Butler, educating their parents on matters of equity yet self-centredly unwilling to cut down their privileges. POST HOPE—the slogan struck me. Could it be a demand in a contemporary landscape that is also the environment of a Last Generation,[10] in which the implications and concept of hope need to be re-read? Questions concerning the natural world can no longer be the subject of hope, as the Anthropocene heads toward extinction. In this respect, there is no alternative to action, since waiting here means losing time to irreversible processes: is hope in the face of melting poles, bleaching corals, and drying fields synonymous with loss?

Käthe Kollwitz, *Tower of Mothers*, 1937/38, Neue Nationalgalerie Berlin.

New Sobriety

When I was small, my parents had three art catalogues on the bookshelf in their shared study in the attic, all of which I had studied meticulously, sneaking upstairs when they were busy. One was a catalogue of prints, drawings, and sculptures by German artist Käthe Kollwitz. I vividly remembered the photograph of a sculpture and recently looked up its title—*The Tower of Mothers*. This was perplexing because nothing about the work seems remotely reminiscent of a tower. A small piece, only measuring under 30 cm in height, *The Tower of Mothers* from 1939 is a curious example of modernist sculpture. Rather a fortress of skirts and aprons than a tower, it depicts a group of women with strong, emotion-filled expressions and bodies that convey a sense of solidarity and protection. At the skirts' level, we can catch glimpses of children nestled between the bulwark of bodies and fabric. In 1938, *The Tower of Mothers* was removed from an exhibition by the Nazis with the statement claiming that in the Third Reich, mothers would not have to protect their children any longer—the state would do it for them.

The sculpture reflects Kollwitz's political activism and her commitment to promoting social justice. Like other representatives of the Neue Sachlichkeit movement, her art was deeply coined by experiences of the First World War and the ensuing crises. Neue Sachlichkeit, or New Objectivity, was a predominantly German phase in literature, music, and visual culture during the turbulent Weimar years 1918-33. In the visual arts, it was most prevalent between the mid-1920s and early 1930s. Although 'New Objectivity' has been the most common translation of Neue Sachlichkeit, other translations have included 'New Matter-of-Factness', 'New Resignation', 'New Sobriety', and 'New Dispassion' as the original German term in its specific nuances cannot be captured in a single English word.[11] Some of the movement's famous representatives are Otto Dix, Lotte Laserstein, Jeanne Mammen, and George Grosz. It was a recurrence of the visible world, emphasising the thing-like through portraits and still lifes, in which realism often would border on the grotesque. Gustav Friedrich Hartlaub, who first employed the term Neue Sachlichkeit, notes in an exhibition catalogue that it "tears the objective from the world of contemporary facts and projects current experience in its tempo and fevered temperature."[12]

Trained as one of the few female painters in the late 1900s, Kollwitz decided in her thirties to abandon colour altogether after reading a treatise by Max Klinger, who stated that black and white techniques were the most adequate form of expression for human pain. Pain and misery of the working class and war-ridden people are at the core of Kollwitz' oeuvre. She had an extraordinary ability to point out social injustices. In 1924, she designed the poster "Nieder mit den Abtreibungs-Paragraphen!" (Defeat the abortion paragraph!) or in 1925 "Mütter gebt von eurem Überfluss!" (Mothers, give from your abundance!)—promoting breast milk banks that helped to defeat infant mortality and foster female independence. Most prominently, however, she depicted the incredible sadness of mothers who lost their children in the war, a fate which she suffered in the First World War, having lost her son Hans whom she had actively encouraged to serve in the field. I get a sense from her work that it depicts a world after hope. This sense is also conveyed in titles such as *Raped, Woman with Dead Child, Mourner, Woman in the Leap of Death, War, The Sacrifice, The Widow, Unemployed, Hunger* and *Child Mortality*. Still, her work is not nihilistic, and when I try to remember the feeling the images evoked in me as the child that could not read the titles yet, I think it was strength.

When describing the work of Käthe Kollwitz, especially her poster-like prints, contemporaries sometimes used the term Tendenzkunst. "*Tendenz* (a cognate of *tendentious* and occasionally translated as 'purpose') was a clear reference to art that is not 'fine art' because it was instrumentalized for political or social ends."[13] Avant-garde artists under the trauma of the war, however, agreed that Tendenz was no longer something to be avoided.

New New Objectivity

I try to practise visualization, and it is really not as easy as it sounds. I know what I want, but for some reason, I cannot reconcile those goals with a halfway realistic vision of a near future. I feel that unrealistic visualization misses the point, even though I begin to enjoy how a thought system starts to unpack itself in paradoxical patterns. Still, I want to be a good student and try harder. Is the problem not my lack of imagination, but the relationship between a present in crisis and its future? Spending my time speculating instead of visualising, I think of how Lauren Berlant questions our fantasies of "the good life" in her book *Cruel Optimism*. She suggests that "lives and livelihoods we have taken for granted" become more and more impossible to attain, and that only by recognizing that these fantasies are fraying can we develop alternative ways of living in the present. "Cruel optimism names a relation of attachment to compromised conditions of possibility."[14] I feel this explains a lot but am in doubt about if it explains my failed exercise. Finally, I go to the studio without yet knowing what I am going to do there.

---

1) Maggie Nelson, *On Freedom. Four Songs of Care and Constraint*, McClelland & Stewart, Toronto 2021, p. 51.
2) Jacques Racière, *The Emancipated Spectator*, Gregory Elliott (tr.), Versa, London and New York 2009, p. 15.
3) Terry Eagleton, *Hope Without Optimism*, University of Virginia Press, Charlottesville 2015, pp. 100-101.
4) Wolfhart Pannenberg, *The God of Hope*, in CrossCurrents, Vol. 18, No. 3, University of North Carolina Press 1968, p. 289.
5) Encyclopedia of Buddhism, https://encyclopediaofbuddhism.org/wiki/Lojong, last accessed April 18, 2023.
6) Terry Eagleton, *Hope Without Optimism*, University of Virginia Press, Charlottesville 2015, p. 84.
7) Friedrich Nietzsche, *Human, All Too Human: A Book for Free Spirits*, Marion Faber and Stephen Lehmann (tr.), University of Nebraska Press, Lincoln 1984, (First published by Charles H. Kerr & Co., 1878), p. 71.
8) See for example: David Harvey, *Abstract from the Concrete*, Sternberg Press, London 2016, or Oliver Wainwright, *Super-tall, super-skinny, super-expensive: the 'pencil towers' of New York's super-rich*, The Guardian, February 5, 2019, https://www.theguardian.com/cities/2019/feb/05/super-tall-super-skinny-super-expensive-the-pencil-towers-of-new-yorks-super-rich, last accessed April 25, 2023.
9) Kaisa Kortekallio, *Turning Away from the Edge of Madness: Kinesis, Nihilism, and Area X*, in Collateral, No. 16, 2019, https://www.collateral-journal.com/index.php?cluster=16, last accessed April 10, 2023.
10) Last Generation: (from German) Letzte Generation is the name of a German and Austrian ecological movement that came out of both Fridays for Future and Extinction Rebellion.
11) Dennis Crockett, *German Post-Expressionism: the Art of the Great Disorder 1918-1924*, Pennsylvania State University Press, Philadelphia, 1999.
12) G.F. Hartlaub, *Ausstellung "Neue Sachlichkeit". Deutsche Malerei seit dem Expressionismus* (Mannheim: Stadtische Kunsthalle, 1925), exhibition catalogue Anton Kaes, et al., eds., *The Weimar Republic Sourcebook*, University of California Press, Berkeley and Los Angeles 1994, pp. 491-493.
13) Louis Marchesano (Ed), *Käthe Kollwitz: Prints, Process, Politics*, The Getty Research Institute, Los Angeles 2020.
14) Lauren Berlant, *Cruel Optimism*, Duke University Press, Durham 2011, p. 24.

Backstage Boo 1, 2, 3

Bod Mellor

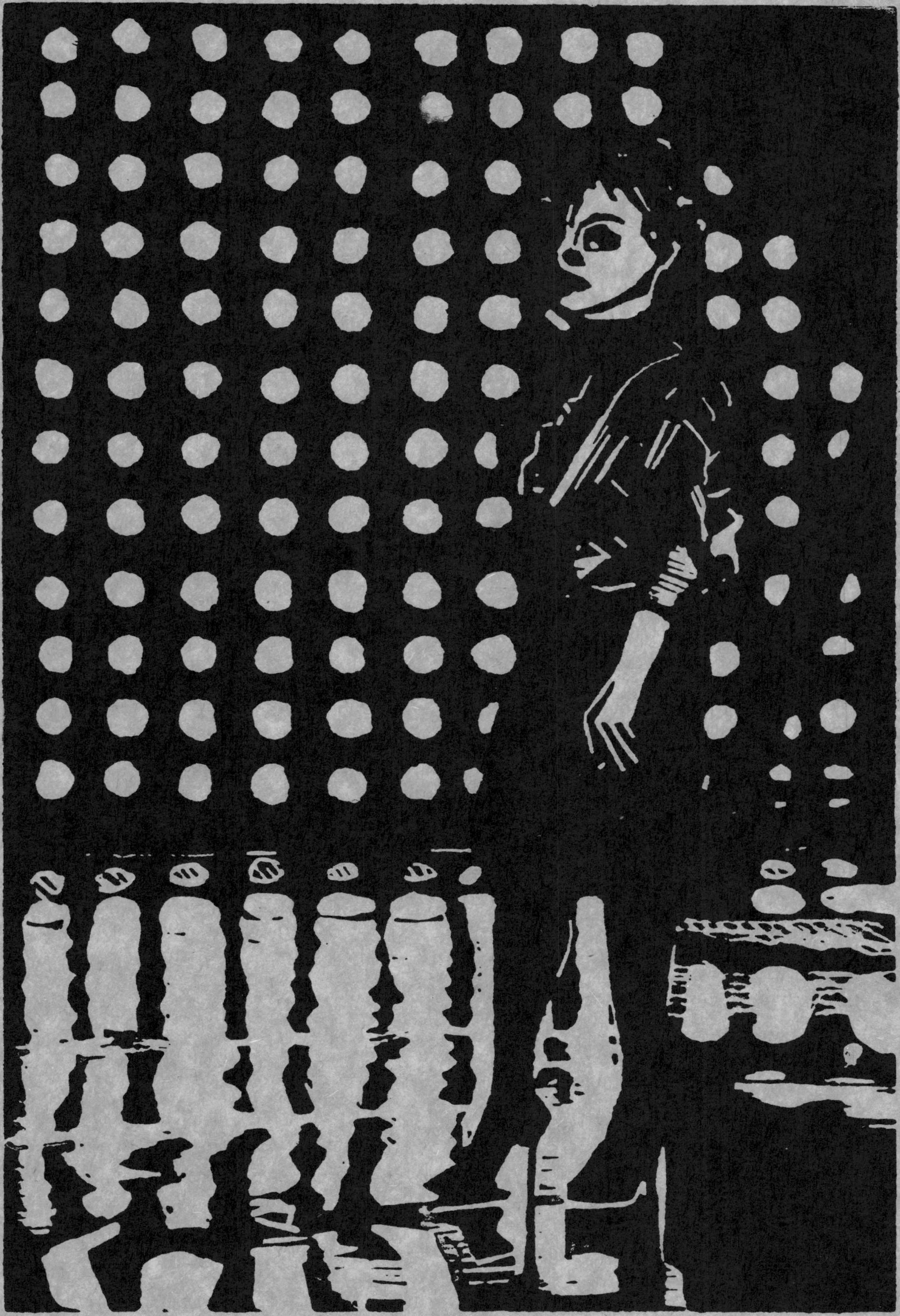

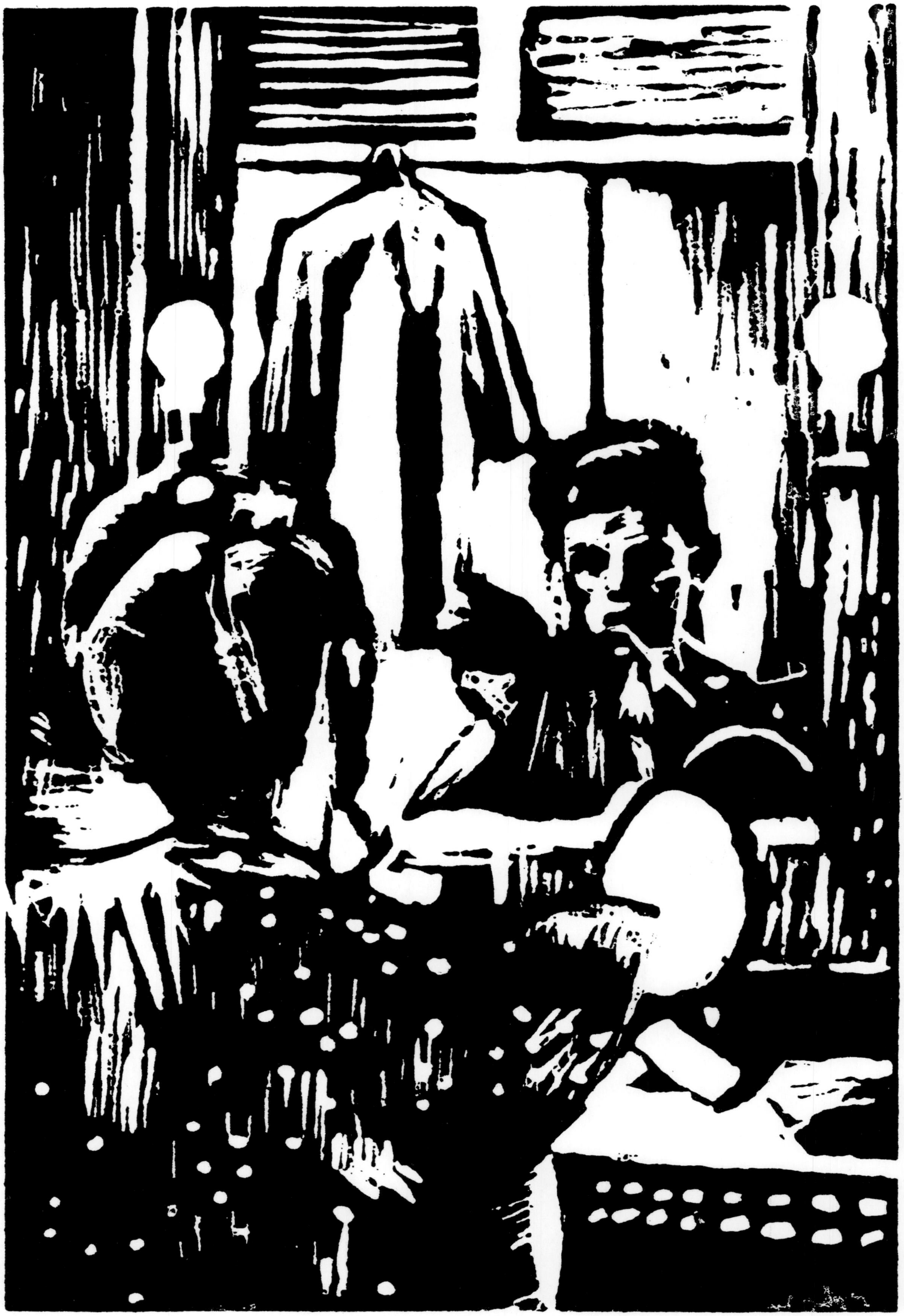

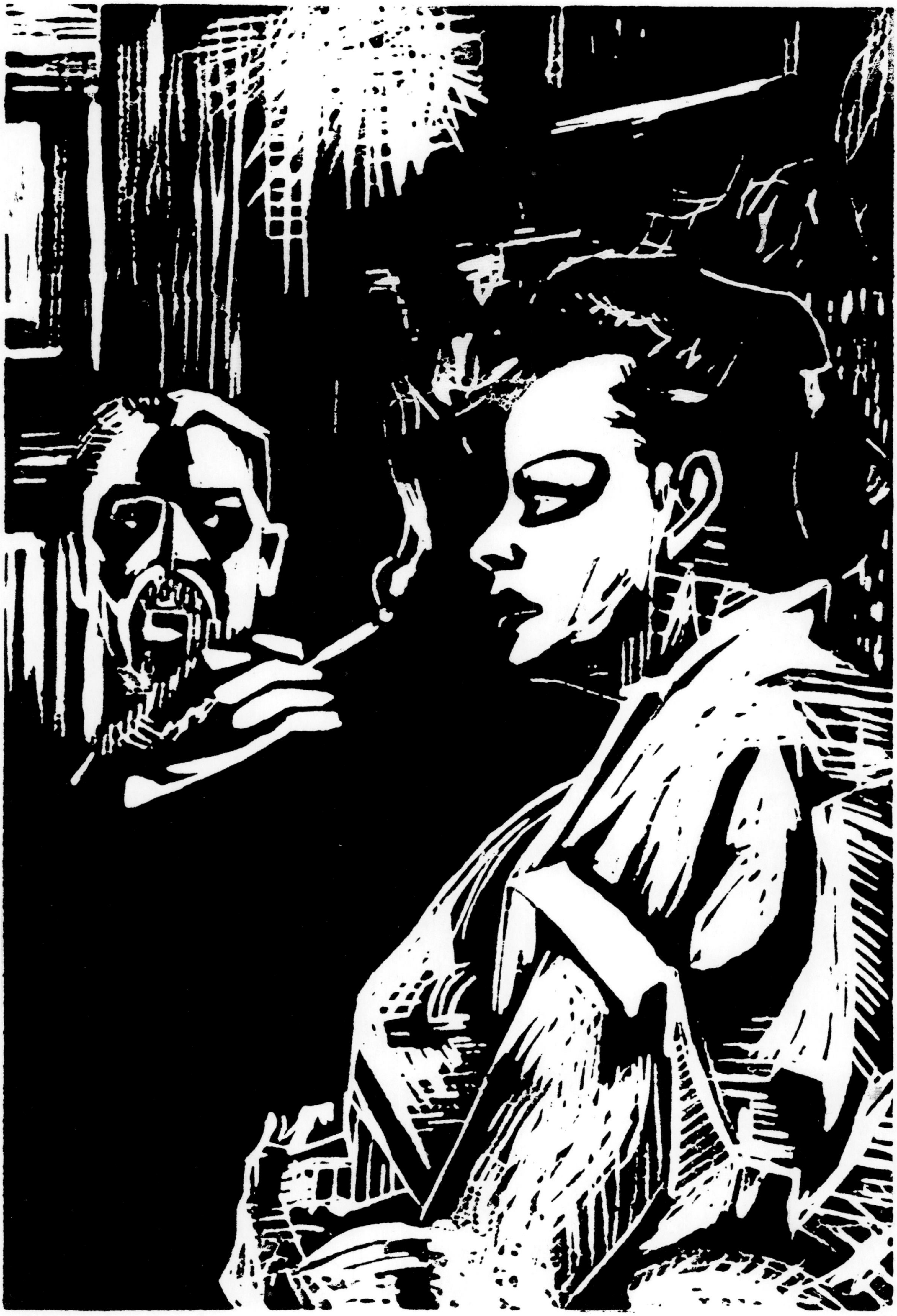

Müde

Moesari

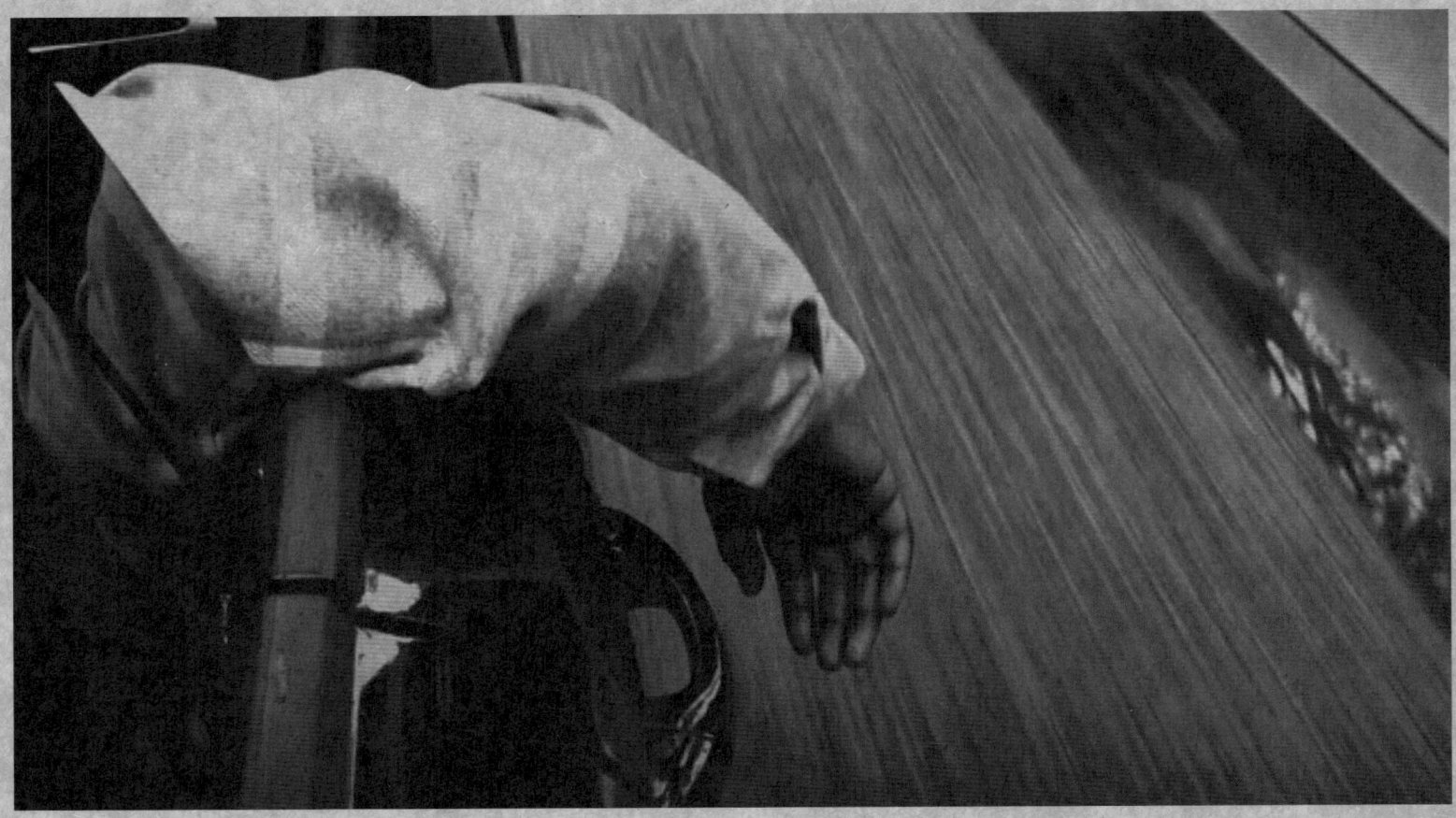

https://www.youtube.com/watch?v=VXsUxeQdTIA

The Weak Lips of a Woman

Cordula Ditz

A beautifully formed small hand rose up from an opening in a dining-table and gave me a flower; it appeared and then disappeared three times at intervals, affording me ample opportunity of satisfying myself that it was as real in appearance as my own. This occurred in the light of my own room, whilst I was holding the medium's hands and feet. You cannot perceive this *Something* violently; go past the grasp of the mind that measures all things except this *Something*. You cannot perceive it with concentration. Keeping the purer eye of your soul turned inward, you should extend an empty mind toward this *Something* in order to comprehend it, since it exists outside of the mind. Everything in the universe exists in a state of vibration. It's all about the frequency at which it vibrates. All things in the universe are made up of energy. Quantum science shows us that at the subatomic level, everything is pure energy that is in a constant state of motion, or vibration. The speed at which it vibrates is its frequency, and different things vibrate at different frequencies. We are vibrating at a different frequency than the air we breathe or the paper you hold as you read this. Even things that appear to be solid and unmoving are vibrating. Their subatomic particles are bouncing around all over the place, at a level at which we can't see, so for us, the object appears solid. The frequency at which matter vibrates governs the form that the energy that makes up matter will take. Everything has its own frequency. It's true, some things have similar frequencies. For example, each of the tables at the coffee shop vibrates at about the same frequency. They're all similar tables. After all. But each person – in physical form or not – vibrates at their own frequency. Table turning was derived from an ancient method of divination through spiritual agencies (*mensa divinatoriae*) and in nineteenth-century usage the idea was that the vibratory movements (transferred to the table at the behest of spirits) indicated certain letters of the alphabet, sometimes written down, at other times shouted aloud by the medium. In this way the table turner spelled out messages supposed to come from the spirit world. Woman's Day was celebrated at Lily Dale on Aug 22nd 1894. Over 2.000 people arrived on the regular trains, and presumably another 1.000 upon the excursion trains. Flags and yellow ribbons and buntings were floating from porches, balconies, and windows-an every place where there was room to put them. Chairman Barrett opened the session by a well-worded address of welcome to the suffragists who had come to Cassadaga for their annual celebration. He said the suffrage movement was born the same year and simultaneously with the Rochester knockings, the beginning of Modern Spiritualism, and that Spiritualism embraced every movement that for liberty and equal rights. Spiritualism began to take shape in 1848, the very year and in the same area of New York State that gave birth to the organized women's rights movement with the Seneca Falls Convention. In July 1848, seventy-two years after the American colonies declared their independence from England, a handful of American women called a meeting in Seneca Falls, New York, to declare independence from the "absolute tyranny" of men. Some 300 participants in the first Women's Rights Convention debated the merits of a document they called a Declaration of Sentiments. Consciously modeled after the Declaration of Independence, the text called on the U.S. Government to grant its female citizens, "all the rights and privileges" already enjoyed by white American men. The passage from earth may be symbolized by a river. From the earth side the waters look dark and angry, running swiftly between high banks. But from our side the river looks like a small crystal stream, with inclined banks, lined with beautiful angels waiting to greet the comer. None are afraid to cross from the spirit side, but you are afraid to launch out from the earth shore. January , 1864., a seance with Miss Colburn was held in the Blue Room of the White House. Several socially prominent guests also attended. Miss Colburn went into a deep trance, as was the usual procedure. When the young medium regained consciousness at the end of the sitting, she was surprised to find that the other guests had left the room, and that the President and Mrs. Lincoln had been there alone with her during the last half hour of the seance, conversing with spirits. The meeting now being over and the medium normal and awake, the President thankfully shook her hand and expressed his gratitude for the service she had been to him that evening. "My child", he said, "you possess a singular gift. That it is of God I have no doubt. Thank you for coming here tonight. It is more important than perhaps anyone here can realize." Lincoln had made up his mind. The next day he signed the Emancipation Proclamation. Spiritualism is threefold; it is scientific, philosophical, and religious. It must be built on the rock of truth, not on the sliding sands of superstition. It's not the believe in a historical God or a geographical God. It's the believe in an eternal and infinite one—A God that is too large to be put within the covers of a book. The revelation altogether too grand to be compassed by any human idea. Mrs. Colby had no new arguments, she said, to bring forward, but would as a few words to strengthen the faith of her hearers. She was assured of woman's progress every time she heard of a woman's day, a woman's union or a woman's club. Men spend far more time in telling women what they can't do than helping them to do it. They say, "see what you have accomplished without the ballot. We have done this for you." They forget how opposed they were to the innovations they now praise. The condition of women in Germany, who performed manual labor while yoked with oxen or harnessed with dogs, or those in the far East, who dared not walk the streets unveiled was scarcely more deplorable than patriotic working women of America, who were governed without consent and taxed without representation. Buckley at Chautauqua recently laughed at the idea that women were slaves, "Jesus said nothing to Martha about being a slave." But on the other hand, neither did he say anything to Lazarus about being a slave. Yet if the learned doctor were occupying the same position as Lazarus did, he would be apt for rebel against it.

It was in 1872 that the first Presidential nomination went to a woman. Victoria Woodhull, beautiful, eloquent and 34, was already a national figure. She and her sister had come out of a childhood of squalor in Homer, Ohio, to score sensational successes in Wall Street as "the world's first women brokers" and "queens of finance." Victoria used her own newspaper and lectures, which drew thousands, to keep herself in the limelight, and to shock Victorian America. She boldly proclaimed, "Yes, I am a free lover." She preached Spiritualism. She sharply criticized capitalism. In the early 19th century, a married woman could not sign contracts, was not entitled to her wages, did not have legal custody of her children, could not own property, could not attend college with men, and she could not vote. In the public sphere, when a woman married, she was without rights. He has made her, if married, in the eye of the law, civilly dead. **The public, however, was growing eager to paint a sexualized picture of the pair as they became more public. Their background as spiritualists was also shady to Wall Streeters, as the practice was sometimes associated with prostitution. They would use money, earned from the brokerage firm to fund the suffrage movement, and Victoria Woodhull would come to be known as the first woman to petition for women's suffrage in front of Congress. Victoria later said, "We went into Wall Street, not particularly because I wanted to be a broker ... but because I wanted to plant the Flag of women's rebellion in the center of the continent." Victoria Woodhull was nominated as the US presidential candidate for the Equal Rights Party. Her vice-presidential candidate was Frederick Douglass, though he never acknowledged it. Victoria tried again in 1884 and 1892 for the US presidential nomination.** The gendered modes in which Spiritualists claimed religious authority provided was the means by which the practice was demonized and marginalized by nonbelievers. It was precisely the negative, feminine coding of medium-ship that shaped a cultural understanding of Spiritualism as irrational and connected it with excessive, uncontrolled sexuality that later allowed doctors recategorize the medium as the hysteric. While most religious groups viewed the existing order of gender, race, and class relations as commanded by God, Spiritualism was associated not only with the women's rights movement, but also with the abolition of slavery and other radical movements. At a time when no church ordained women and many forbade them to speak in the house of worship, and women were considered merely the property of their husbands or fathers, women in Spiritualism had equal authority, equal opportunity, and held high religious office in equal numbers. Many mediums gave lectures in trance under the direct influence of spirits. These trance speakers were the first group of American women to speak publicly before large mixed-sex audiences. The sexes were thought to have opposite electric poles. The negative charge of women made them attractive to the positively charged (male) spirits. This gave the female mediums an advantage because only they could receive the messages of the significant male spirits. Thus, they made political speeches under the influence of spirits of such famous personalities as Napoleon, Socrates, and Benjamin Franklin. Since it was not they–but the spirits speaking through them who were responsible for the content–the women could not be held liable for it. Not very surprisingly, the rights of women were now suddenly very dear to these spirits after their deaths. Spiritualism flourished at a time when the dominant culture, informed by science and medicine, was working overtime to fix the boundaries of maleness and femaleness–and later, homosexuality and heterosexuality–and solidifying those binaries as natural, essential, and immutable. Victorian women, cast as both pious and passive, could claim mediumship as a natural calling. Quite different questions and connections are raised by the fact that a significant number of men would find a parallel power in receptivity, crafting an unconventional model of masculinity through spiritual mediumship and trance speaking. That both Spiritualist men and women could reimagine their gender through practices ranging from cross-dressing to defying the vocal ranges equated with sexual difference suggests yet another world of transformations. **Spiritualism's loose structure makes it problematic to say all spiritualists believed one thing or another, but the movement adhered to two critical tenets; an emphasis on the value of individuality; or the equal value of each soul or person, and the idea that after death people entered spheres of spirituality based on the degree to which they had respected the individuality of others while they had been alive. "The only religious sect in the world that has recognized the equality of women is spiritualism," wrote women's rights leader Elizabeth Cady Stanton. Spiritualism peered women opportunities to expand their roles as leaders without overtly confronting 19th-century expectations.** I was holding the medium's two hands in one of mine, whilst her feet were resting on my feet. Paper was on the table before us, and my disengaged hand was holding a pencil. A luminous hand came down from the upper part of the room, and after hovering near me for a few seconds, took the pencil from my hand, rapidly wrote on a sheet of paper, threw the pencil down, and then rose up over our heads, gradually fading into darkness.

Jan Matthé

Two by two, tracking, what to do with content? Tolerance flourished, faces awake with assumption and secrets. It promised interruptions, communion, mist, musical scores. Will it arrive, absolute pleasure? The staying awake, the keeping the gift warm. Mind seeking body—eggs alive—silent and slow, in the middle of touch. Forever unknowing. *Forget the intent, forget the whole story.* [Sent to S.D.S, 8400 Oostende, 13.4.23]

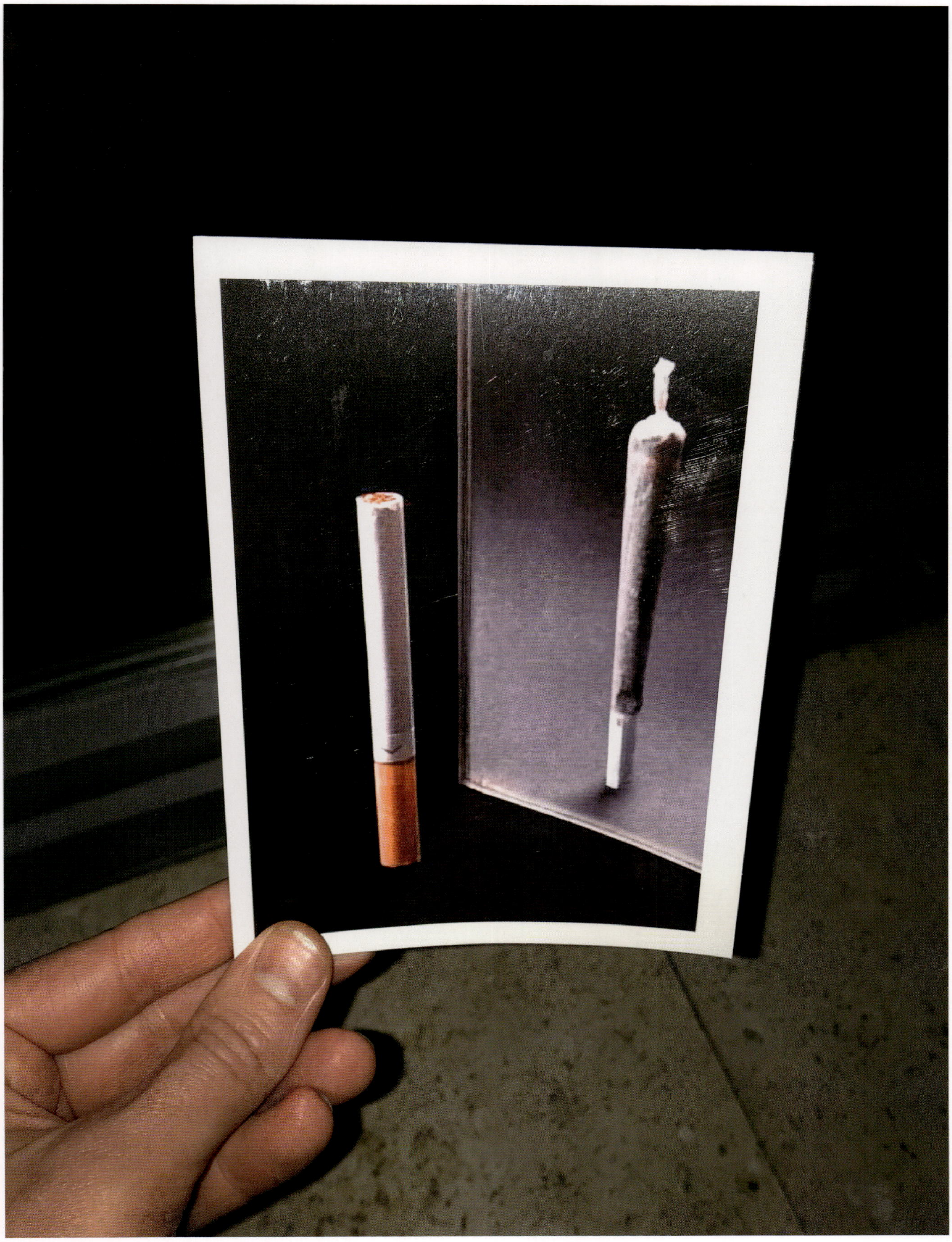

About Turn, Resounds, Decays

Katy Lewis Hood, Leah Jun Oh, Jac Common

IV. As the thing that's heard

When we got there we couldn't listen to the thing we wanted to. Three concentric circles. In the wharf reinstalled at the tempo of development and then abandoned again nothing sounded *as/like* a bell for opening time/the land for loot. Jem Finer's *Longplayer* in a lighthouse, started the last moment of the last century and meant to last—never repeating, never overlapping—for a 1,000 years.

∞

The 234 'singing bowls' in *Longplayer* are kinds of standing bell—probably originating in China but re-marketed in the 1970s via US 'new age' music—'which can be played by both humans and machines, and whose resonances can be very accurately reproduced in recorded form.' Scores of precision ripples, still in movement materials can't be predicted. *Longplayer* is 'designed to be adaptable to unforeseeable changes in its technological and social environments, and to endure in the long-term as a self-sustaining institution.' Yet when J asked a security worker if they could open up the lighthouse for us, we never made it up the spiral stairs.

I. Evasive
listen,
what's surrounded & withheld as
sensation is   a practice of exclusion—
not ambient, instrument or antenna—
an otherwise—   overwhelmed by the world—
troubled
cleft, bracelet-weight
antennae
          adjust gestural waiting
     in attention
not aplomb
but moving the linguistic terrain of perception
          a bit
     bytes blur at edges
attuned as insects
trace each other's trebled over-
laps heard
whirling-floating, downfacing-or-upright

IV. (As the thing that's)

What would have happened if we *had* been able to listen, supervised by the security worker? Would we also have heard his labour time watching us in that tubular space of exchange—an interruption in our interruptions of each other, a fourth person in the tension of listening. The durations would alter. Now?

∞

Later J will have played one singing bowl somewhere else, experimenting with how striking certain parts of the metal changes the pitch at which the bowl is resonating. The sound will be unbearable to L. For hours in nights afterwards I listen to *Longplayer* stream live from the lighthouse with the locked door in my ears, imperceptible as time units in duration without

II. Manoeuvres of sensation
     pitch. in spirals.
as of flowthrough.mode coagulate. s.
          lips dissolve over it.boundaryfoldf.low it.with.ing. the point of glance.redo.redo
     drifts. in a way of distort
          infinite behinds of geometry.s.now
as heightened.ing arcs as
sound bows   sense.able the flows
.flaws.
     a hyper.circle
.ing between.fingertip
as heightened attention as

      shaking off
evasive environments
.other elements
in order
distilled.concentrating
in rings.all the way down
the height of it.
      undo.undo
time
notes show
edges in
another dimension

III. Refuse the question
but who could dance to this?
bell inverted from hold
   held absorbs directly struck objects
      flattens kept vibrations

            Every step is heavy, unless light as a stutter. —only,

234 singing bowls
install vibes vaguely "ancient"/
the texture of instrument discarded as launchpad
each note played a scrape
in its own gradual warping

heap disform iteration
   (a lapping over it) down to abyssal plain of human hearing
     ~20Hz   sub-octave
boundaries of noticing. adjusted to press
under low lapse of sound, a far flung spiral arm
plays like insects finding footholds   the same iteration of one infinity   :how motion
kind of meanders to distraction
the spiral, in
peripheral, like
an erosion of your edges
unfocus, or suspicion of concentrating
upon an infinite point:
call it
skittering on a crystal cave ceiling
      ~20,000Hz   super-octave
call it
   shook off time

At extremes of scale
passing on quantum mechanical levels and expanses no more than a blip. isn't to say tonality in
which we flicker as little particles / nothing
    only everso ahistorically /
only upright / only stacking

Hear chime, think "instance," it continues to wobble
     after peal. overtones. pulse. each
    minute increment. metal distunes.
:||Repeat for 1,000 years.

Botanomancy

Paige Emery

Choose a plant to sit with / let the plant choose you
Introduce yourself (polite new friend) / thank the plant (gift aware)

Inhale the visual signature of the plant
Exhale the pressures of time
Inhale the aroma of the plant
Exhale expectations
Inhale the essence of the plant
Exhale the need to rationally explain

Ask a simple question that needs guidance
(if your question is complex, retract it to how it got there and to how it got there and to
    how it got there until you reach a root—the root holds the question)
Sit in sensory communion, open like flowering petals in your chest, listening for guidance
Listen for guidance in dancing shapeforms, distant murmurs, the threading of disparate points
Thank the plant (tender gift) and take it with you in your memory

Recent Dreams

Alejandra López

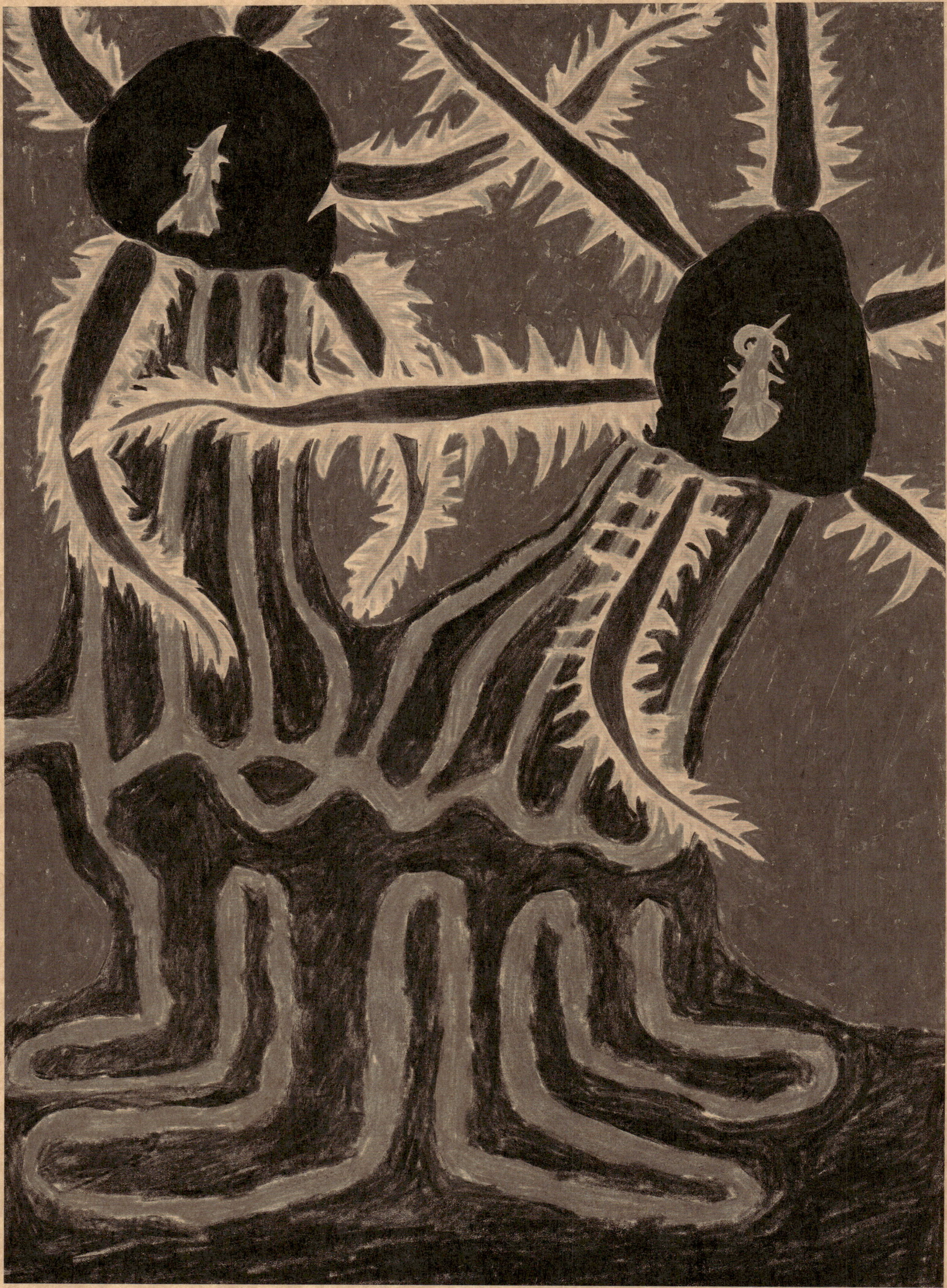

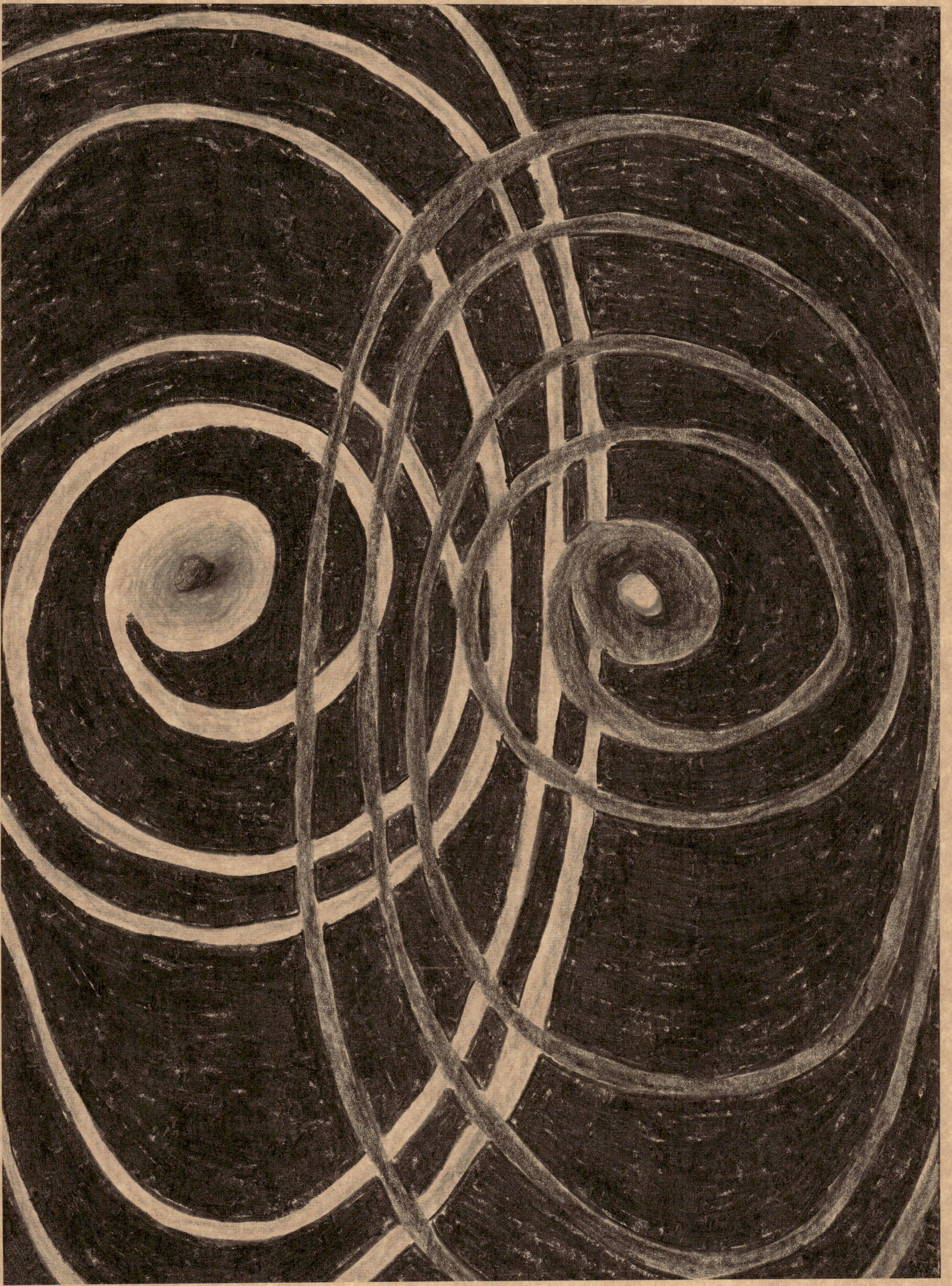

Unruly Women on Planes, Nameplates, and Goats

Nina Kuttler

Sabiha Gökçen Airport in Istanbul is small compared to the new airport on the European side of the city. There is never a free place to sit, an outlet to charge a phone, or a fountain to refill a bottle. Named after the first female fighter pilot, it is one of 16 airports in the world named after a woman. Of those, only three of those names belong to aviators, or aviatrices: Amelia Earhart Memorial Airport, Aitchison, USA; Jacqueline Cochran Regional Airport, Thermal, USA; and Sabiha Gökçen International Airport, Istanbul, Turkey.[1]

As one of Atatürk's adopted children, Sabiha Gökçen had access to education and the opportunity to choose to become a pilot. While attending Tayyare Mektebi (Aviation School) in Eskişehir, she received special training in a plane that had been modelled to fit her size. Sabiha was the symbol of the modern Turkish woman. And to be the world's first female military pilot,[2] to be of Turkish descent, and additionally to be one of Atatürk's adopted daughters, made her life story a source of national pride.[3] Having landed and flown from Sabiha Gökçen Airport multiple times in the last year, I wanted to be proud of Sabiha, too. I wanted to celebrate and admire her for achieving what no woman had achieved before her, despite all obstacles, gender stereotypes, and glass ceilings. I wanted her to be the hero for women's rights she is portrayed as, and I wanted her to join the ranks of all the other women who achieved, first, what they were perfectly capable of—even specifically gifted to do—despite the obstacles and social restrictions thrown in their paths.

Sabiha was the symbol of a new Turkish society: modern, open to the world, offering equal opportunities to women. When I mentioned my interest in her story to a friend in Istanbul, it was immediately met with slight resentment. Not only was she a flying woman, but also the only woman to take part in military operations during the Dersim rebellion, making her the first Turkish female air force combat pilot. During this military operation, numerous bombs were dropped on the Kurdish people in the Dersim region rising up against the government. Despite her role in paving the way for Turkish women in aviation, she took part in popularising oppression and violence against Kurdish people. Even though I want to celebrate her and the other women mentioned in this piece for their achievements and talents, I also wonder: why is it special when women fly?

The list of women aviators and their achievements on Wikipedia is long: Leman Altınçekiç, first female accredited jet pilot in Türkiye and NATO; Tamar Ariel, Israel's first Jewish female religiously observant air force pilot; Asli Hassan Abade, first African female fighter jet pilot; Jean Batten, first solo flight from United Kingdom to New Zealand; Amelie Beese, first woman pilot in Germany; Willa Brown, first black woman to hold both a commercial and private licence in the USA; Mary Calcaño, first Venezuelan woman to be granted a pilot's licence; Pearl Laska Chamberlain, first woman to solo a single-engine airplane up the Alaska Highway; Jerrie Cobb, first woman to fly in the Paris Air Show and to be tested as an astronaut; Hélène Dutrieu, first woman pilot in Belgium and to carry a passenger (who caused a sensation by flying without a corset); Amelia Earhart, first woman to fly solo across the Atlantic; Lotfia Elnadi, first Egyptian woman to earn her pilot licence; Rose Lok, first female Chinese-American pilot in New England; Ruth Law Oliver, first woman pilot to wear a military uniform and the first to deliver air mail to the Philippines; Ingrid Pedersen, first woman to fly over the North Pole; Vera Zakharova, first Yakut woman pilot.[4] This is just a fraction of the aforementioned list. There is no such list for male aviators; there is a list of aviation pioneers.

In folktales, mythologies, legends, religious, and pagan belief systems, flying women—witches, fairies, harpies, swan maidens, goddesses like Hekate, Diana, Nike, etc.—are uncanny, unchained, sexual, uncontrollable, loose, fierce, savage, sometimes willful, always untamed creatures, often possessing the ability to shapeshift. Lilith, the primordial she-demon in Judaic and Mesopotamian mythology, borrows the shape of an owl, or even disease-bearing wind. As the archetypal (sexually) untamed women, she is the flying nightmare of millennia-old patriarchal societies. In Jewish mythology, Lilith is the first wife of Adam. But unlike Eve, she was made simultaneously with Adam and therefore is his equal. She is the first unruly woman—breaking free from domestic restriction—and therefore the first monstrous-feminine.[5]

Greek and Roman mythology imagines harpies as winged female creatures, alternately described as beautiful maidens with wings, bare breasts, and sharp bird-like claws, or terrible flying monsters with ugly faces pale with hunger, equally bare breasts and predatory claws and wings ready to steal children from the face of the earth. In Edvard Munch's drawings titled *Harpyie,* dark-haired flying bird-women with almost angelic wings but seemingly razor-sharp claws are shown plummeting to the ground ready to swoop up a skeletal half-dead figure.[6] These images evoke similarities to vultures but with serenely calm facial expressions, perhaps even carrying their prey to heavenly salvation. Nevertheless, malicious flying witches and harpies alike are a product of patriarchal fantasy and fear of losing control and superiority. Equally, witches and harpies are somewhat sexually charged figures. The medieval idea of a witch is a lecherous, unchaste woman who engages in sexual acts with the devil.[7] This licentiousness speaks to the misogynist's worst fear: unruly women living free of restriction.

In mediaeval Europe, ideas about Lilith and classical-world flying monstrous-females, such as Harpies, Circe, and Medea, began to mix with European folk stories and the relatively new Christian church still trying to replace Paganism. The European witches

---

1) *Fairports,* https://www.netflights.com/c/airport-hub/airports/fairports/, last accessed April 17, 2023.
2) Here it is important to note that in fact the French pilot Marie Marvingt was the first female pilot in combat. She flew medic flights during WWI and served in the military disguised as a man, *Viewpoint: Why are so few WW1 heroines remembered?,* BBC News, October 27, 2014, https://www.bbc.com/news/magazine-29706831, last accessed April 17, 2023.
3) "You have made me very happy... Now I can announce what I have planned for you... Perhaps you will be the first female military pilot in the world... You can imagine how proud it would be for a Turkish girl to be the first female military pilot in the world, can't you? I'm going to take immediate action and send you to the Aeroplane School in Eskisehir, where you will receive special training." (Mustafa Kemal Atatürk), https://web.archive.org/web/20141006181638/http://www.hvkk.tsk.tr/tr/IcerikDetay.aspx?ID=34&IcerikID=86, last accessed April 17, 2023.
4) *List of women aviators,* https://en.wikipedia.org/wiki/List_of_women_aviators, last accessed April 17, 2023.
5) Serenity Young, *Women Who Fly,* Oxford University Press, New York 2018, p. 158.
6) Edvard Munch, *Harpyie,* 1899, Lithograph, Munch Museet Oslo.
7) Kristen J. Solleé, *Witches, Sluts, Feminists,* Stone Bridge Press, Berkeley 2017, p. 23.

moved outside the rule of men over women and God over men, and thus were scapegoated for everything inexplicable and mysterious which, at a time without any significant medical treatment outside of bloodletting and herbal brews, was a lot. Most frequently accused of witchcraft were unmarried women living in rural areas outside of any domestic context, midwives, practitioners of pagan rituals and women with knowledge in herbalism. In the dualistic system in which the Christian church classified all of society—everything inside the clerical framework equals good and everything outside of it equals bad aka the devil—these unruly women had no space within the church. The publication *Der Hexenhammer (malleus maleficarum)* written by Heinrich Kramer elucidates the misogyny that eventually led to witch persecution, particularly in Germany and other Christian parts of Europe.[8] According to the self-proclaimed witch hunters, European witches used domestic items—cauldrons to boil and eat babies and broomsticks or pitchforks to fly and engage in orgies with the devil—to practise witchcraft. Witches were commonly thought to manufacture a sort of flying ointment out of any number of things, including the scraps at the bottom of a cauldron from above mentioned infant soup. This ointment could be directly spread on the naked body, or on an animal, such as a goat, or on objects, like a broomstick. The ability to fly was especially significant as it enabled witches to break free from social conventions and domestic life. Witches flew to freedom and out of the control of overbearing husbands, brothers, fathers, or neighbours.

The actual ability to pilot a plane—to fly—still holds a powerful symbolism of freedom for many women. Another unruly woman in that sense is Niloofar Rahmani, Afghanistan's first Air Force pilot. According to her autobiography *Open Skies*, even as a child she expressed the wish to become a pilot, when, during a walk with her father, she observed a commercial plane fly overhead. At the time, this seemed like a practically impossible path for a woman in Afghanistan. Later, during the brief period of relative freedom for Afghan women after the Taliban regime was forced out in 2001, she was able to attend school, university, and, in spite of resistance from almost all sides, became Afghanistan's first fixed-wing pilot.[9] Joining the military was the only way for Niloofar to fulfil her wish of becoming a pilot. After completing pilot training, she completed cargo flight and transported injured soldiers. Despite successfully completing pilot training, becoming an officer in the Afghan Air Force, and working for years in the Afghan military, some of her male colleagues failed to accept her as equal, and she and her family also received threats.[10] A woman who wears a uniform, a woman who fights for her rights, a woman in charge is something many men in contemporary Afghanistan—especially the younger men who grew up under Taliban rule—are still not used to.[11] A woman who defies her supposed domestic role and becomes a pilot presents an uncanny threat to the patriarchal rule. The growing anger Niloofar and her family were constantly confronted with finally led to her and her family fleeing Afghanistan.

Patriarchal societies operate on a double standard when it comes to things like the ability to fly or practise magic. Even before the big wave of witch hunts, from 1400 on, there were plenty of male ritualistic magicians who deliberately evoked demons and controlled them. But with the massive losses in population, quality of life, and security after the prior outbreak of the Plague, the climate of despair gave way to the above-mentioned dualistic world view split between good—the Catholic Church—and evil—the devil, or everything outside of the clerical frame.[12] This blend of distress, hardship, and bigotry was just right for the rise of the malicious witch. Those accused of witchcraft were for the most part female and were believed to be possessed or under the control of demons.[13] Daedalus, who in the Greek legend builds wings for himself and his son Icarus allowing them to fly, is described as a skilled craftsman. Therefore the flight, despite it ending in Icarus' death and becoming a metaphor for human hubris, is perceived as a result of competence, not an alliance with the devil or some other evil force. By that logic, the European witches who were said to have been brewing flying ointment and applying it to simple household items like broomsticks in order to enable them to fly, could have equally been perceived as competent and skilled instead of in a pact with the devil.

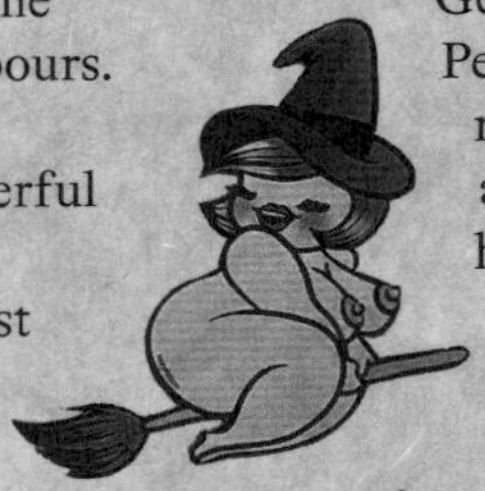

Generally, male-coded mythological figures such as Pegasus, Cupid, or the Centaur are connoted with rather positive virtues such as courage, romance, and strength, whereas Harpies, sphinx, or witches have something uneasy and malevolent about them. Whenever female figures are airborne, they are unpredictable, ungovernable, and often badly intentioned. Therefore, when women fly it is uncanny, dubious and menacing; when men fly it is gracious, dignified, and awe-inspiring.

The history of human aviation in the last 150 years or so has been male-dominated. Female pilots are the exception, and were previously often referred to as *aviatrix,* in distinction to the male form, *aviator*. Women in aviation were also frequently called condescending nicknames such as *ladybirds*, *angels,* or *sweethearts of the air,* and were almost always referred to as girls rather than women.[14] (The evolution from old hags to girls is hardly a sign of progress in this fight for equality.) Equally frequent was the blame put on technical difficulties when a male pilot crashed, while a woman crashing her plane was proof that women simply were not cut out to fly.[15] During her pilot training, Niloofar felt the pressure of representing not just herself but all Afghan women. Any mistake on her part would not be seen as a personal failure but as testimony for all Afghan women's ineptitude.[16]

To this day, flying women, now simply known as pilots, are not the norm. However, since the invention of mechanical flying devices, witchcraft could, with almost total certainty, be ruled out as an aid in female flight. So, what is it now that is perceived as uncomfortable about flying females? This contemporary discomfort about female flight is a symptom of the slowly crumbling patriarchally organised society whose dust is being whirled up in the wings of unruly women like Niloofar Rahmani.

8) The thoughts expressed in *Der Hexenhammer* are neither new nor obsolete. One example in contemporary media is convicted rapist and human trafficker Andrew Tate, who expressed similarly misogynistic ideas to millions of followers via his social media channels until these accounts were banned in 2022 by platforms such as TikTok, YouTube, and Facebook.
9) Before the Taliban rule there were female helicopter pilots in Afghanistan: Latifa and Laliuma Nabizada. *Latifa Nabizada – Afghanistan's first woman of the skies*, BBC News, June 19, 2013, https://www.bbc.com/news/magazine-22943454, last accessed April 18, 2023.
10) *First female Afghan Air Force pilot speaks out about her experience in the military,* CNN, https://edition.cnn.com/videos/world/2021/07/23/first-female-air-force-pilot-afghanistan-acfc-full-episode-vpx.cnn, last accessed April 18, 2023.
11) Niloofar Rahmani with Adam Sikes, *Open Skies: My life as Afghanistan's first female pilot*, Chicago Review Press, Chicago 2021, p. 199.
12) Kristen J. Sollée, *Witches, Sluts, Feminists*, Stone Bridge Press, Berkeley 2017, p. 22.
13) Serenity Young, *Women Who Fly*, Oxford University Press, New York 2018, p. 166.
14) ivi, p. 233.
15) ibid.
16) Niloofar Rahmani with Adam Sikes, *Open Skies: My life as Afghanistan's first female pilot*, Chicago Review Press, Chicago 2021, p. 170f.

So, was Sabiha Gökçen an unruly woman? As a child she demanded to be educated beyond the level considered appropriate for women at the time. She voiced this wish with confidence when Atatürk visited her hometown, and she was subsequently adopted by him. This secured her path in higher education and later, a career in aviation.[17] Despite being an advocate for women's equality and smoothing the path for Turkish women in aviation, she was also very much part of a politically motivated plan and served as an instrument to showcase Turkey as a progressive nation.

Women as commercial pilots today are indeed a familiar occurrence but are still underrepresented in this area; the global average for women pilots is 5.8% with India's national average at the top with 12.4%.[18] I am also looking towards Christina Koch, the only woman on the Artemis mission to land on the moon in 2024.[19] Space travel lends an additional meaning to the term *flying*, but it is equally vital to insist on equal opportunities for all genders in this area too.

Being unruly means instigating change and progress, and insisting on emancipation and (r)evolution. In that sense, this is an encouragement to be unruly: a witch, a harpy, Niloofar, Circe, Lilith, an aviatrix, even a fairy or a ladybird. These labels speak of the fear towards, and power within the symbol of liberated, uncontrolled (airborne) women. To proudly be such a woman means reaping the fruits of the labour and suffering of generations of feminists, witches, and unruly women before us.

In parts of the world influenced by the West, witches have been popularised by countless books, movies, and TV series. The term *witch* is an example of a formerly derogatory term for women—along with its canine cousin—that is being reappropriated and turned into something powerful, desirable, and representative of self-determination by (Western) women.[20] Likewise, mythical creatures such as fairies can be seen in positively connoted roles. In the neo-noir, steampunk series *Carnival Row*, the character Vignette Stonemoss is courageous, savvy, vigorous, and she is part of the airborne faes. She is headstrong, a fighter and a leader, definitely a threat to the oppressive system, and an unruly woman. Personally, I would happily refer to myself as a witch. Admittedly, I get a queasy feeling whenever I am on a plane leaving the Earth's surface. Maybe that would be different on a pitchfork or backwards on a goat—they seem like more reliable means of flying to me.

Flight symbolises freedom of movement and consequently freedom in a broader sense. In this vein, I see women in aviation not as a side note of the general history of aviation but participants in a broader fight for equality. Accomplishments achieved by women in flight are landmarks on the pathway to a future where everyone can move and live their life however they wish.

17) Melahat Simsek, *Geburtstag von Sabiha Gökçen, türkische Fliegerin und erste Kampfpilotin der Welt*, SR2 Radio, March 21, 2023, https://www.sr.de/sr/sr2/sendungen_a-z/uebersicht/zeitzeichen/20230321_sabiha_goekcen_sendung_100.html, last accessed April 18, 2023.
18) René Bocksch, *Frauen sitzen nur selten im Cockpit*, Statista, August 11, 2022, https://de.statista.com/infografik/27970/frauenanteil-unter-pilotinnen-in-der-kommerziellen-luftfahrt/, last accessed April 18, 2023.
19) Patrick Klapetz, *Diese vier Artemis-Astronauten fliegen 2024 zum Mond*, mdr Wissen, April 4, 2023, https://www.mdr.de/wissen/raumfahrt-das-sind-die-vier-artemis-mond-astronauten-100.html, last accessed April 18, 2023.
20) Kristen J. Solleé, *Witches, Sluts, Feminists*, Stone Bridge Press, Berkeley 2017, p. 13.

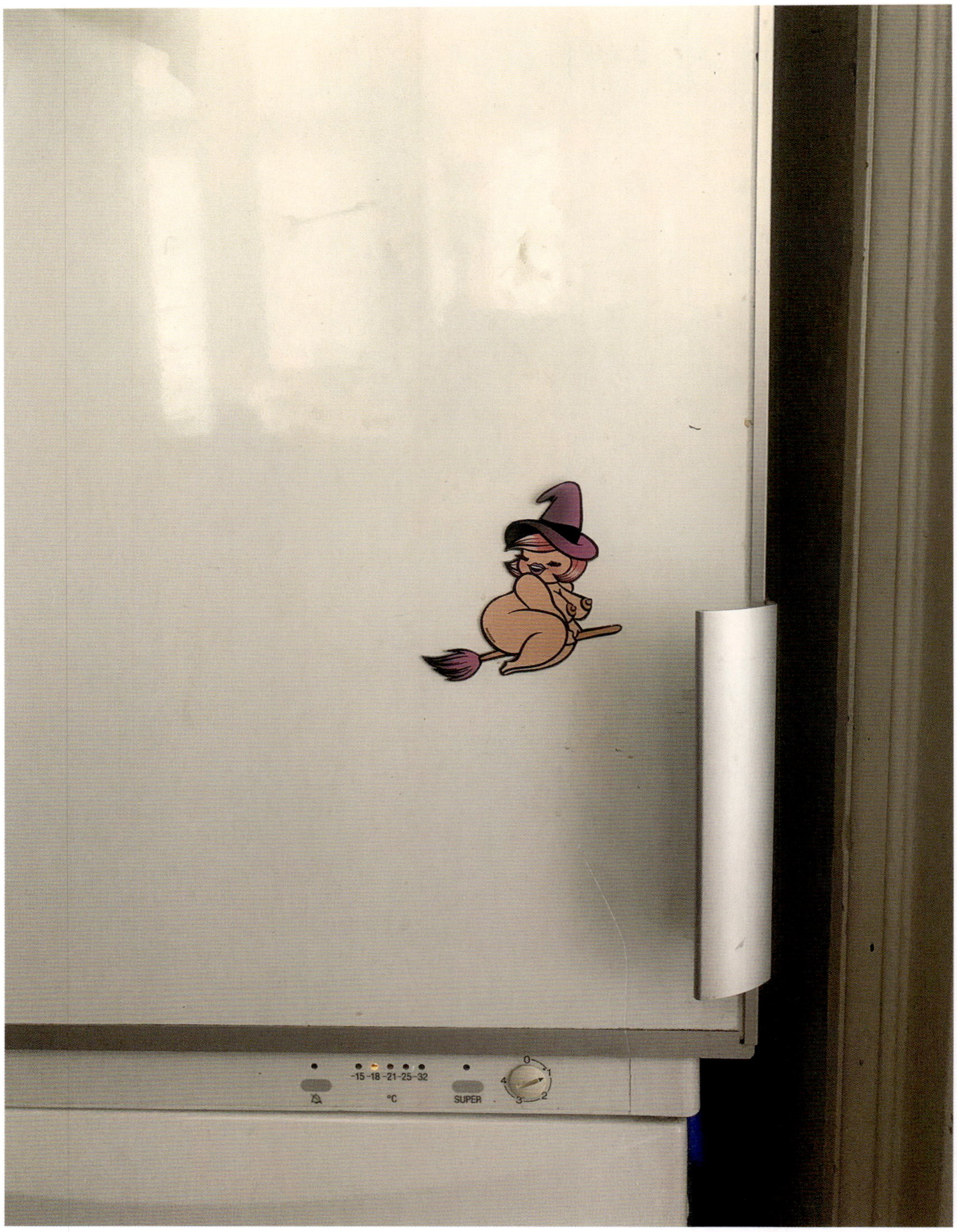
-15 -18 -21 -25 -32
°C
SUPER

9 783945 247273